Lost and Found:

Losing my memory, finding myself

SARAH BERGMAN

DEDICATION

To my supportive and long suffering husband, Ben, who promised to love
me no matter what and kept his promise.

ACKNOWLEDGMENTS

I praise God for his awesome provision and healing. I am so thankful for the loving church family and community He has provided. I would like to thank my husband Ben and my daughters, Lauren and Carolyn, for being more wonderful to me than I could ever hope for or deserve. Thank you Kathy Kerber for your encouragement, advice, and awesome editing skills.

Thank you to Scott Bade, Cheryl Wren, Heather Nygaard, and Jennifer Nehr for taking care of me when I couldn't take care of myself. Thank you to Sean and Amanda Calvert and Patrick and Alysia Buob for taking care of my children when I was away in Seattle. Thank you to all the people who brought our family food during my recovery. It was delicious.

CONTENTS

CHAPTER 1

Running allows me to set my mind free.
Nothing seems impossible, nothing unattainable.
– Kara Goucher

I am a runner, although I hesitate to describe myself that way. I would hate to give you the wrong impression. I would hate for you to imagine someone on the cover of a running magazine, a spindly, lithe young thing, with a flat, ripped mid-section exposed by a little sport bra style top and tiny nylon running shorts, waistband rolled down to the hip bone. That would not be me. I've never actually seen my abdominal muscles as they have always been protected by a generous layer of subcutaneous padding. Even if I could see them, I would keep them covered; I wouldn't want to make anyone feel bad.

I will not be joining those elite athletes standing at the start line of a race, holding my foot up to my butt cheek, stretching my quads until just before the starting buzzer sounds. You will find me about a half mile behind those people, fully covered in moisture wicking fabric, adjusting the ear buds of my MP3 player, waiting for my corral's turn to start the race. I'm not there to win anything. It will take twenty minutes of shuffling forward before I even reach the starting line.

After the crowd thins, you will find me contentedly trotting down the road, scanning the backs of the runners in front of me. I'm looking for a target to follow, a partner in the race, or a person to beat to the finish line. My focus is to finish the race feeling good about my efforts and without the need for medical intervention. You will not find me qualifying for the Boston Marathon or featured in a running magazine.

I don't run because I'm good at it. So why do I run, if nothing is chasing me? Although I hate to admit it, I am plagued by vanity, that little voice in my head telling me, "You can do better than that, can't you?" and comparing my reflection with the images I see in magazines and television. Every once in a while, I think to myself, "If I weren't me, I'd think I was a nice looking person." I try to talk to myself like I would a friend, with kind and encouraging words, but soon the voice of vanity returns.

I would never say to a friend the things I let that voice say to me. It whispers reminders to not become one of those overweight housewives that let herself go, much to the dismay of her husband. It tells me that if I wear pajama bottoms or sweats in public, people will think I'm lazy and careless. It instructs me to color my premature gray hair and use moisturizer with sunscreen so that I won't look older than I am. Vanity demands that I must look fresh and young, despite the fact that I get older each day.

The thing vanity torments me the most about is my size. It tells me that as a woman, I should be fragile and delicate. I should be light enough to be carried over a threshold like the brides in movies. A strong man should be able to lift me into the air like a ballerina or a figure skater. I shouldn't be the same weight as a man, even though I come from a long line of substantial women. I should be small.

I know in my heart that none of that is true and yet I swing on a dizzying pendulum between dissatisfaction and contentment. I look back at pictures of when I was younger and I am angry with myself that I wasn't kinder in the way I evaluated my body. I was too harsh and would have enjoyed life more if I had only given myself some grace and acceptance. I'll live in that place of liking myself the way I am until I put on a pair of pants I haven't worn in a while and struggle to button the top or I see a reflection of a large, round woman in a shop window and realize it's me. It scares me into action.

The voice of vanity competes with the voice of sanity, the one that tells the truth. While one says I should be thin and delicate, the other says I should be the best ME I can be, strong and healthy. I thought running would help me with vanity's goal because runners are generally thin. Turns out that thin people are just more likely to run. Running didn't make them that way, but it does answer the call of sanity to be healthy and strong. Though vanity convinced me to start running, sanity kept me going.

I started exercising slowly, walking mostly at first and then gradually running more than walking. The first five minutes were always the worst, but it got easier as time passed. Once I got passed the initial discomfort of the pressure of my feet pounding the pavement and my lungs starting to tighten and burn, it started to feel good. My muscles gained definition and my breathing slowed down. I felt free and powerful. I added distance to my running routes. I started entering racing events, which helped motivate me to continue running on a routine basis. I had to train so I wouldn't feel like the walking dead afterward. Running became part of who I was.

No matter how far I ran, I stayed roughly the same weight. I lost about six pounds when I first started and the needle moved no further. I was told that running is a great weight maintenance tool but to lose weight, I would need to restrict my calorie intake by eating less of everything I like. An unfortunate side-effect of running is increased appetite. After a long run, I felt famished. Calorie restriction sounded like waterboarding to me. Rather than torture myself, I learned to accept my body for its endurance and stamina, if not its size. Running stopped being about some unachievable goal of changing my body type and became something I did to maintain my mental and spiritual health.

Running cleared my mind and calmed my spirit. Eric Liddell said in Chariots of Fire, "When I run, I feel [God's] pleasure." When I ran, I felt a sense of security, strength, and well-being. It is as though I was lifted from a fog of turbulence into clear skies where problems that were once complicated and ambiguous become defined and manageable. For a time, my vanity and all the fear and anxiety it produced melted away. The power of exercise silenced that nagging voice in my head.

In times when I felt angry or frustrated, I could run and return home feeling calm and reasonable. I replayed conversations in my mind and put myself in the other person's position. I let the negative emotion seep out of my pores like the sweat dotting my forehead and I wiped it away. Without a critical internal dialogue, I could commune with God and hear the voice of truth in my mind telling me who I am in Him, His beloved child, loved and accepted just the way I am.

That's not to say running was all rainbows and lollipops. One winter, I slipped on a patch of ice on the sidewalk and caught myself just before my face made contact with the cement. In the process, I pulled a leg muscle so badly it hurt to even walk. After a week of limping, I followed a friend's advice and made an appointment with a chiropractor.

At my first visit, the doctor explained how chiropractors use manipulation to restore mobility to joints restricted by tissue injury. He noted that every professional sports team has a chiropractor on the sidelines to immediately aid athletes after an injury. He then showed me a special ultraviolent light he would shine into my leg muscle. Studies had shown that with multiple treatments, it would accelerate healing, he explained. I asked how long before I could run again.

"These kind of injuries usually take between six and eight weeks to heal. Maybe sooner," he predicted. I wanted to get back to running so I figured I'd do what he asked and see how things went. He asked me to lie down, lifted each of my legs, and slowly put them down again.

"You definitely have a lot of tightness in your hip joint," he commented. Before I knew what he was doing, he took my injured leg by my foot and yanked as hard as he could. It might have hurt if I hadn't been in complete shock. My leg did feel better when I walked out of his office, but I could still feel a faint soreness.

I went back three more times for the flashlight treatment but it didn't seem to do much. My leg healed after six weeks, just like he predicted, but I'm under the suspicion that it would have taken that long no matter what I'd done. That first yank of my leg made a difference, but after that, I probably could have stayed home and rested.

The reason I continued treatment was because I wanted to feel like I was doing something to aid my healing. I never thought to myself that I should quit running, that it wasn't worth the pain. I wanted to get better as soon as possible so I could get back out on the road again. I missed the way running made me feel, mind and body.

As much as I enjoyed my solitary runs, making plans to run with a friend helped me stay consistent and recover from my injury.

I'll admit, when I first met my running partner I was skeptical that we could be friends. Blonde and beautiful, she had the long and lean body that I could never have. Feeling a tinge of jealousy, I imagined she had an eating disorder to be so thin. Then she got pregnant. As her body softened, my heart softened too. Maybe we could be friends after all.

We gradually got to know each other as we led worship at church, played board games on Saturday nights, and shared potluck meals. It didn't take long to realize she didn't have an eating disorder, but a fast metabolism and naturally slim frame. She seemed oblivious to her beauty and embarrassed by compliments about her figure. She could have been proud and arrogant, but she was the opposite. When I mentioned that I had started to run, she offered to join me and a wonderful partnership was born.

I'm so glad I didn't miss out on knowing her because of my superficiality. My gracious friend, a woman who could be pictured on a running magazine, insisted she was as out of shape as I was. She never made me feel inadequate or slow. We scheduled times to run each week and held each other accountable to run even if one of us wasn't in the mood. We both needed the chance to unwind and decompress; Having a set time kept us from ignoring that need. Gradually increasing our distance and pace, we decided to run a marathon. Her friendship gave me the encouragement to do more than I thought was possible. What a blessing.

Because she had small children, (including a nursing baby) we couldn't get together more than once or twice a week. I tried to find another running buddy, but it wasn't easy. I had a couple other friends who would run with me. One liked to take frequent walking breaks and finish after a few miles. I enjoyed visiting with her but felt held back in my workout. I tried another friend who worked at the local gym teaching weight training classes. She was fit and strong, but exercised mostly in the gym. She mentioned that she'd like to start running so I asked if she'd like to join me. I thought with the extra time I had put into running, she and I might run at a similar pace. No such luck.

With a short, quick stride, she would consistently run a couple paces ahead of me. It was hard having a conversation because as I tried to keep up, she would speed up. Finally, I would get tired and go back to a pace I could maintain and she would ask, "Is this the pace you normally go? This feels slow to me." It made me feel like a slug. I thought I could take it, but my self-esteem couldn't handle the blow. I decided I would rather run alone than feel inferior, so when my original partner wasn't available, I ran solo.

I clipped an article from a running magazine and loosely followed its training schedule for a marathon. Because of the weeks I couldn't run due to my injury, I fell behind on increasing my mileage over time. I decided not to run the full marathon, but the half instead. My friend stayed in the marathon and though we didn't run the race together, we motivated each other to the starting line. Race day in June gifted us with perfect running weather in Seattle, overcast and not too warm. The whole experience felt incredible. I was one of thousands of people filling the streets as far as the eye could see. I walked to the starting line to see my brother and sister-in-law who came to cheer me on, and noticed those elite runners with their freakishly thin bodies contorted into pre-race stretches. All jealousy evaporated. I didn't want to be with them. I was happy to join the pack behind them and embrace the experience of being part of a mob, running through parts of the city unknown to me.

The whole experience felt like a game of tag. I picked a person to watch and I weaved in and out of the crowd to reach them. Once I caught him or her, I found a new target. Near the end, the finish line became my sole focus as I watched the hoard of people in front of me turn the corner to the final stretch. I finished in two hours and 13 minutes, maintaining my goal of a 10 minute mile. I was pleased and ready to run another ½ marathon, shooting for less than two hours next time. Feeling motivated to keep my training going, I went home and researched up-coming running events in the area.

Runner's World magazine featured an article on the best races across the country. Listed as the race with the most waterfalls, the article featured an event held on November 3, 2012 on the hiking trails of Silver Falls State Park near Salem, Oregon. Conveniently, it was within a day's drive of home. I immediately made reservations for a cabin at the State Park for the nights before and after the race. I had to wait a couple weeks for the event registration to open.

The day I was supposed to register, I forgot to stay awake until midnight to get on the website. I remembered in the morning, but by then it was too late. All the slots for the ½ marathon had been filled. Spots remained in the marathon. I already paid for the cabin and I didn't want to lose that money or watch other people run, so I registered for the full marathon.

That's how I started training for my first trail marathon. I wasn't fulfilling a life-long goal or checking off an item on my bucket list of things to do before I die, but I thought why not? I could say I had done it, even though it's hard to prepare for a run through a rain forest with elevation changes of 5000 feet when you live in a relatively flat terrain with a desert climate. I followed a training schedule and hoped for the best.

As I trained for the marathon, I mostly ran alone. My running partner had a hard time leaving her four kiddos with her husband at bedtime and I trained in the evenings. I missed her company, but I created a soundtrack of music to keep my mind focused and my body moving in a forward motion. On Sundays I ventured on long runs and my husband Ben rode his bike beside me and carried water bottles to keep me hydrated. His encouragement helped me keep going when my feet started to ache and my bra rubbed me raw.

Our family traveled from our home on the dry side of the mountains to Silver Falls State Park on the wet side. When we arrived, rain poured all day and all night, leaving the ground saturated with water. The trails turned into ponds of muddy water in places and obstacles like tree limbs and rocks littered the course. The Oregon sky filled with so many heavy, gray clouds that it felt like a giant wet blanket, blocking the sunlight and pressing down on the earth. The cold permeated skin and muscle, settling in the bones.

As I listened to the pounding of rain on the cabin roof instead of sleeping, I second guessed my choice to run a marathon in a rain forest. I pictured myself trekking the woods shivering, wet and cold. Those thoughts haunted my dreams. Fortunately, I woke to a morning sky that threatened rain, but didn't follow through. It merely hid the sun and cast a gray hue on the lush, green landscape. I loitered near the back of the pack of runners, knowing I would not be among the first to cross the finish line.

I struck up a conversation with a nice man in his 50s who had run the ½ marathon in the park previously. He warned that the end of the course was brutal and that he hadn't been prepared his last race. He advised me to take it slow and have fun. Starting the day with friendly small talk reminded me why I enjoyed organized events. Running with others produces a magical feeling of cosmic connection. I appreciated the encouragement and started the run in good spirits.

For the first six miles, the race felt casual and easy with soft breezes, birds chirping, and the sound of rushing water in the distance. The crowd had not yet thinned and the path held only minor obstacles like the occasional mud puddle or fallen branch. We reached the first water station and the pleasant jog through the woods came to an end. The trail became a steep grade up the first of many nearly vertical hills, and as we began the ascent, the run transformed from a leisurely jog to arduous climb. I started marching, like I was climbing a mud staircase. It is easy to jump over puddles on level ground. It's tougher to jump while climbing uphill at a steep grade. I did what I could to avoid the deepest water holes and not fall down in the process. I started running again when the trail went downhill or level.

At mile thirteen, I thought I could stop running right then and feel pretty good. I had been running for two and a half hours and I was ready to be done. Unfortunately, 13 more miles of course laid ahead, with trees, mountains, and waterfalls standing between me and the finish line. I waited in a short line for a toilet, reasoning that I should use it before I really needed it, just to be on the safe side. Apparently the person before me actually needed it because she took a good five minutes.

As I waited, I watched my pack of runners leave me behind. I made it out of the portable toilet, stopped holding my breath, and looked to the top of the steep climb that towered above the valley where the parking lot and restrooms laid. Little figures trotted across the skyline at the top. A string of people followed behind, climbing the rocky slope. I turned up the volume of the music playing on my iPod and decisively plodded up the grade, hoping to reach another straggling runner.

Those miles included the toughest climbs I've ever experienced. Head down, watching for potential hazards, I methodically plotted one foot in front of the other. Water soaked through my shoes from fording through a stream that could not be bridged or by-passed. I could feel hot spots forming on the tops of my toes. Two of the runners ahead of me sported super hero costumes, complete with capes. I watched the ground to navigate the trail but frequently lifted my head to track them. I used them as my target until we reached level ground when I passed them. I didn't see another runner for the next six miles. Alone I climbed more forested mountains, wondering how much distance I had covered.

Unaccustomed to climbing, I over-estimated my progress. When I reached the point where I thought there should be a rest station, I found only a waiting park ranger, telling me I'd reached the highest elevation and that the rest station was only three miles away. It had taken me an hour and a half to go three miles. I had anticipated it taking half that long, not realizing how steep the climb would be. It took me another forty minutes to get to the next water station, which by that time, I desperately needed.

Feeling starved, I popped open an energy gel pack and sucked down the gooey sweetness. It met my immediate need but I wasn't sure how long its effects would last. With nearly eight more miles to go, I had yet to see anything worthy of a postcard. In the past four hours, I had accumulated more water in my shoes than I had seen falling scenically from the mountains I had climbed.

Temporarily revived, I let loose and allowed gravity to take control. As I pounded down the slope, I felt something pop in my shoe. I thought it was a toe nail because it felt like there was something floating around in my sock. It didn't hurt any worse than before but I tried to imagine what my foot must look like. I pictured a bloody mess and a vulnerable pink stub where my toe nail should have been. I started getting a sick feeling thinking about it so I tried to focus on something else.

The run down the mountain took a lot less effort than the climb up it, but my poor knees ached from the extra force of falling forward. A negative internal voice came to taunt me. "Why are you doing this again? You are so stupid," it told me. I turned up the music to tune it out. Every runner has mantras they recite to get through the dark times, a little saying to help them continue putting one foot in front the other. It's easy for me to listen to that critical voice and get discouraged so I prepared little sayings to keep me going like, "Just keep swimming," and "Remember the water falls!"

By the time I got to the waterfalls, I didn't care to see them anymore. I had been running for five hours in a dark, damp mountain forest with sore, soaked, and possibly deformed feet. After running under the largest waterfall, the trail led me to a stair case of over a hundred steps. I thought, "If there is a literal hell, this must be what it's like." The trail had been opened to the public, so I passed people in street clothes on the path as I grunted up the stairs, plodding one foot in front of the other. I didn't feel like much of a runner at this point. I just wanted to be done. My mantra had deteriorated into "Just let this be over already."

After that grueling climb, I entered the home stretch. My family waited for me in an open meadow directly across from the finish line. They clapped and waved as the trail took me up one last hill and dropped back down into the valley where the race ended. Completely spent of all my energy, I trotted across a little foot bridge to the finish line in the field where the race began. It had taken six hours to complete the race, far longer than the five hours I had hoped for.

By the time I crossed the line, there was no hot food to be had; only boxes of the puniest apples I had ever seen. A race organizer walked up to me as I loaded my arms with apples, determined to take as many as I could. He asked if I'd like a race shirt. "Sure," I said, happy to get a free memento. Too bad I can't eat a shirt, I thought as I waited.

The organizer told me that even though they knew the course would be challenging, they had no idea the rain would make it as technical and challenging as it had been. Elite runners crossed the finish line with blood running down their legs, saying it was the hardest course they had ever run, far more difficult than they anticipated. I think he was impressed that an over-weight housewife-type like me finished the race. There were still thirty people left on the course somewhere and fifty had dropped out.

My family and I returned to our cabin in the park after the race. Luckily for me, we packed bread, peanut butter, and jelly and after inhaling a couple sandwiches my growling stomach felt satisfied. I gingerly untied my shoes and pulled them gently off my feet. My drenched socks stuck to my feet like glue, but their color sported no blood red, only muddy white. I slowly peeled and shed the socks from my feet like a wet second skin, and to my relief I found all my toe nails fastened to their respective toes.

My big nail looked a bit bruised but firmly attached. What had made that popping feeling as I pounded downhill was a blister between my big toe and pointer toe that had burst. The skin moving back and forth had felt like a nail brushing against my tender toe. It wasn't as bad as I thought it was, but it wasn't pretty.

Despite the blistered toes and sore muscles, I recovered quickly from the day's journey. It didn't inspire me to sign up for another marathon, but I was glad I could say I did it. I finished, even if it took six hours. And I learned a few things from the experience.

First, I learned that running is largely a mental sport. What that voice in your head tells you makes a huge difference in the way you perform, running or not. This is where listening to words of truth make all the difference. It is easy to have a positive attitude when circumstances are pleasant and there are other people around to give comfort and encouragement. It's harder when alone on a rough road, listening to the voice inside. What it says makes all the difference. I can't listen to the lies of negativity and be successful. I have to remember the truth; I'm strong and I can do this.

Secondly, I learned that I can tolerate almost anything as long as I know it's temporary. As long as there was a caped runner, a rest station, or water fall to provide a goal, I mustered the strength to press on. Sometimes it is best not to live in the moment if it is one filled with pain, weakness, or frustration. It can feel like a permanent condition. In order to push through the pain, I have to focus instead on the positive emotions that will come from accomplishing a difficult course. What kept me going was pushing the discomfort out of my mind and focusing on the hope of relief at the end of the race.

Lastly, I learned that the grass is greener on the west side of the state because it rains ALL THE TIME. If it isn't raining, it's because it just got done raining or it's going to rain soon. I've decided that instead of signing up for running events in green places, I should enjoy the desert landscapes of home where the sun shines and the trails are not covered in water and mud. I require the light of sunshine. No more day-long runs through mountainous rainforest parks for me. I'm sticking to wheat fields and vineyards from now on.

CHAPTER 2

One of the pitfalls of childhood is that one doesn't have to understand something to feel it. By the time the mind is able to comprehend what has happened, the wounds of the heart are already too deep. — Carlos Ruiz Zafón, The Shadow of the Wind

In addition to battling vanity and running marathons, I pour myself into caring for my family. With no career ambitions or desire to work full-time outside the home, I decided that when we had children, I would make our family my occupation. My husband's mother acted as the center of his universe during his childhood and he liked the idea of a wife that filled that same role. I happily agreed but for a different reason. The center of my universe died when I was nine, leaving me floating in space with nothing to orbit.

Our history shapes us into the people we become. As much as I'd like to say I wouldn't change anything about my life, I can't do it. I understand that my history produced my character and resiliency, it also plagued me with detachment, loneliness, and insecurity. I wanted to do all I could to keep my children from feeling those things. Recognizing the gravity and importance I would have as a mom, I planned to be intentional in my parenting and not repeat the mistakes of the past.

Much of what happened when I was a child was no one's fault. As Gus said in the movie, The Fault in Our Stars, "Life is not a wish granting factory." We do our best to make it through. When I was born, my parents already had an established family with a ten and eight year old, a farm house they built themselves, and a farm-based bee keeping business. I was a surprise, a mostly pleasant one. My earliest memories are of watching my mom do housework and being put to work doing chores if I complained of being bored.

Living in the country, there wasn't much television to watch and no other children to play with. I lived inside my head, pretending the weeds in our side yard were part of a jungle and there were wild animals living in them. I talked to my stuffed animals and had imaginary friends. I still complained of boredom and managed to do a fair share of dusting and vacuuming, even as a preschooler. I have pictures of me at age four cleaning the house.

I was initially excited to start school when I turned five, joining my older brother and sister on the big, yellow bus that picked us up each morning across the street from our house. At last, I could be where the people are! My excitement quickly waned when I realized I had to sit still for four hours next to kids my age and not talk to them. I got in trouble for being disruptive and resorted to bringing a stuffed animal from home for a listening ear. The teacher sent my animal home.

My older brother thought it fun to try to teach me algebra and vocabulary words like rigor mortis. (We'd play a game where he would yell "Rigor mortis" and I would freeze, stiff as a board, like a dead person. It was great fun.) I only mention this because having this advanced education provided by my warped sibling made Kindergarten excruciatingly boring. It seemed like training for being unnaturally sedentary and disengaged. Those already primed for passivity by television may have fared better, but it was torture for me, which is why when my kids turned five, I didn't put them in Kindergarten.

The end of that first year of school brought two major traumas: a diagnosis and a move. My dad decided to move his beekeeping business to North Dakota and my mom received a diagnosis of breast cancer. Despite the seriousness of her disease, the plan to move remained in place. She entered the local hospital and doctors performed a radical mastectomy of her left breast. Once she recovered, our family packed all our belongings and moved to a tiny town near the Canadian border called Crosby, ND. During the months that followed, mom drove the 132 miles every month to Minot, ND for additional treatment for the next year.

My best memories of our time in North Dakota are of the times I spent with my mom. Some days, she let me go with her to Minot. We ate breakfast together (happy face pancakes), bought snacks for the road (marshmallow peanuts), and enjoyed each other's company. My jabbering kept her awake on the road and I relished the opportunity to skip school. As I look at my first grade report card, I missed over 20 days that first semester. Somehow I still passed and to this day, I love a road trip with good company.

We didn't spend all my missed school days driving to the hospital. Sometimes we'd just stay home together. Mom started working a graveyard shift at a local nursing home in order to help with the family finances. She chose that shift so that she could be home in the morning to get us ready for school and home in the afternoon when we got back. She tried to sleep while we were away, but I don't think she ever got enough. I remember going down to her dark bedroom in the basement and rubbing her back while she rested. Sometimes I could get her to pay me a quarter. Other times we played a game where I would draw letters and pictures on her back and she would guess what they were. Then she would fall asleep.

If ignoring cancer made it go away, she might have cured herself. While sick, she cooked, cleaned, shopped, and cared for our family and worked outside our home while we slept. She continued to do everything like nothing was wrong. Dad worked 12-14 hour days trying to keep his beekeeping business going after a competitor poisoned his hives. He too developed health problems during this time because like Mom, he was overweight, overstressed, and overworked. Needless to say, there wasn't much time for family fun or recreation.

As a seven year old, I spent an exorbitant amount of time alone, watching television. By this time, we lived in a rental house in town and ordered cable television. Over the summer, I consumed it like a starved person, watching from morning to night. I can still remember the episodes of Brady Bunch, Gilligan's Island, and the Adams Family that played every afternoon on the Turner Broadcasting Station. I still cringe to think of all the brain cells I killed at such a young age.

When I finally bored of television, I played in the alley behind our house, pretending it was the road to a faraway land. I started walking further and further from home. Soon I was wandering the neighborhood like a stray dog. I realized that it didn't matter if I stayed close to the house or not, no one was paying attention. My sleeping mother probably thought my teenage brother or sister was watching me, but I don't remember seeing them much. Both in high school, they stayed busy with their own pursuits. Once or twice, Mom woke up and I got in trouble for not being at home. There was no one to tell when I wanted to go somewhere; I didn't think it was a big deal.

At seven, I wasn't old enough to leave a note, but in my mind I felt old enough to go to the store alone. I gathered money from on top of the hot water heater next to the washing machine where my mom emptied pockets. I took it down to the corner store and bought candy or ice cream. The employees there recognized me and learned my name. After years living on a farm, I was used to playing outside, far from the house. Without anyone to stop me, I continued the same habit in town.

That fall, my mom's cancer went into remission and my parents made plans to return to the Northwest. Though North Dakota shared its cold winters and warm-hearted people, it did not make us prosperous or less homesick for extended family. My dad's business went bankrupt and he went to work for his brother. My brother graduated from high school, moved out, and joined the army. My parents lost their farm house that was used as collateral for the business and our family moved into an apartment. Money posed a constant stress and my parents frequently told me we didn't have money for anything special or fun. The tension at home made me want to run away. I sought refuge at school, helping teachers straighten desks or organize papers. I still straighten and organize when I'm feeling stressed.

I remember one cold February afternoon during my 3rd grade year. My cheeks burned dry and red from running in the wind. I pursued my goal of getting home with a singular focus, at the end speed walking with my legs crisscrossed. I burst into the bathroom I'd been waiting to use all day long. The toilets at school flushed violently and loudly so I avoided them at all cost. Relieved at last, I came out of the bathroom and my mom met me in the hallway with a gift in her hand. Her face was pink and splotchy, tears welling in her bloodshot eyes. "This is your Valentine's Day present."

For months, I begged my parents for a Cabbage Patch doll. It seemed like everyone had gotten one for Christmas except me. I held my breath as a opened the package and found a doll: an imitation, home-made doll in the Cabbage Patch style. My heart sank like a rock. My mom didn't understand the status involved with the special stitching and signature on the butt of an authentic Cabbage Patch. She thought this doll would be extra special because she paid a church lady to sew me a one-of-a-kind doll. I didn't get it for Christmas because she hadn't finished it in time. She was planning on giving it to me for my birthday in May but she had received some terrible news.

She explained to me that cancer had returned and spread throughout her body. She would do everything she could to fight it, but her chances of being cured were slim. The doctor told her she may die in a matter of months. My eyes stung as I tried not to wail. The doll wasn't what I wanted but I pretended I loved it for my mom's sake. She wrapped so much expectation into giving it to me, attempting to soften the blow of her devastating news. She didn't intentionally layer disappointment upon tragedy but the sadness was almost too much to bare. We cried together until we ran out of tears and then we kept living, because that's all we could do.

The cancer progressed, attacking Mom's lungs and lymphoid system. It ravaged her body and stole her good humor. She became irritated, short, and mean. A Sunday school teacher reported to my mom that I requested prayer that she would stop being so grumpy. She laughed at the report but my face burned hot with embarrassment. I learned why people make silent prayer request.

Church people talk too much.

One day Mom asked me to bring her a half a glass of water. I went to the kitchen and all our glasses were dirty so I grabbed a cup instead. I filled it to the top and brought it to her. As she tried to take a sip, it spilled on her. "I TOLD YOU TO BRING A HALF!" she yelled.

"I thought a full cup would be the same amount as a half of a glass because it's half as tall," I replied meekly, sad that I failed to follow her instructions.

"The cup is wider. It holds the same amount of liquid," she explained in a softer voice, still tinged with frustration. This was my first and most memorable lesson in the properties of volume. My mom homeschooled me and she didn't even know it.

Mom did extend her life through treatment, dying in November instead of May. It was a long and ugly decline marked with thinning hair, ashy skin, and oxygen tanks. After school started in the fall, our small apartment filled with medical equipment, hospice volunteers, noodle casseroles, and gelatin molds. Mom's sister came to stay with us and well-meaning visitors came to give words of sympathy or support. Long lost cousins came to visit Mom once it was clear she wouldn't recover, prompting her to muse, "Why did they come visit now? They never cared to visit when I was well."

Some friends didn't know what to say and resorted to platitudes about faith and healing. I wanted to yell at them that Mom was dying of cancer, not a lack of faith. Noticing her resignation, some would make comments to my mom about how wonderful heaven is, a place of no tears or suffering. It was like they couldn't wait for the funeral service. This nine-year-old didn't particularly want her mom in heaven, regardless of the pain and tears. Though well-meaning, a lot of what was said hurt more than helped.

For weeks, people swarmed our apartment like bees to a hive. Though the church people sometimes annoyed me, I greatly appreciated the food they brought and the attention given by hospice volunteers offering to play games or build puzzles. My aunt gave me an embroidery project to distract me and my 4th grade teachers gave me special attention at school. I couldn't imagine a world without my mom but I reveled in the love other people gave me.

Once Mom died, the rain showers of love turned to drought. The food, the visitors, and the special attention came to an end, replaced by the new reality of life without my mom. Who would make sure I had food and clothes? Who would do the laundry and clean the house? Who would take care of me if I got sick? Who would sign my school papers and go to conferences? One would think it would be my dad since he didn't die but he had never done those things. That was mom's job. He could hardly take care of himself, let alone take care of two daughters. He didn't hide his brokenness and I didn't know what to do. I prayed to be rescued.

Mom's funeral was in November; my sister would graduate high school in the spring. My aunts worried about me being left alone with my dad so they decided to set him up on a blind date with a widowed friend they knew well. Dad and the widow married six months later, right after my sister's graduation in June. I liked her. I wanted her to be my mom and take care of me but apparently she was unaware that her job description included cooking, cleaning, and watching me. She resigned after two years.

She left us at the end of my sixth grade year while I was visiting my Mom's sister. I found a note saying I could put the things she left behind in a yard sale. I had mentioned to her that I wanted to have a yard sale in order to earn money for summer camp, but I never intended to do it alone. She cowardly left when I wasn't home, left a note, and didn't take me with her. She knew I would be stuck taking care of dad and she would be free. Her leaving hurt worse than my mom dying, because I knew my mom didn't want to go. My step-mother left willingly.

Dad coped with his divorce by entering a dream world of gold and diamond mines that he believed would one day make him a rich man. No one could convince him that he might be wrong about his mining claims. He imagined himself a reincarnated Job of the Old Testament, claiming that God had made him promises and he would wait for Him to deliver.

While I search the kitchen for something to eat, he stared at rocks through a magnifying glass. While I tried to balance his indecipherable check registry, he bounced checks around town claiming, "The Lord will provide." He believed it was just a matter of time before God would restore everything that had been taken away. In the meantime, I had to live in the reality that God might never make my dad's dream come true.

I became more of a peer than a daughter as my dad shared his worries and frustrations. He lamented the inadequacies he feared caused his wife to leave, voiced suspicions that she had an affair, and complained about his meager finances. Every day I heard how we didn't have enough money to pay all the bills and I was taking his last dollar for my lunch money. I hated feeling helpless hearing my dad feel helpless too.

Due to my dad's seasons of unemployment, I moved in with various relatives on both sides of my extended family. I floated from one home to another, attending three different high schools before graduating. Although I enjoyed the academic part of school, I hated the social stuff. Teased about my appearance, my intelligence, and my loud voice, I armed myself with humor and sarcasm. I imagined conversations where I had a witty come back for any insult that was thrown my direction. I used my quick wit and sharp tongue to keep people from getting too close. I acted like I didn't need friends even though I desperately wished I could feel accepted and loved instead of merely admired or tolerated.

I didn't think I would ever get married and have a family. I had such a difficult time surviving the social scene in school, I figured it was because I was deficient in the skills needed to have healthy relationships. No one wanted me. I didn't date or have close friends.

I figured I would graduate from college, get a job, and become a cat lady. Turned out, I was wrong. Someone did want me, wanted to get married and have a family with me, and it was more than I dared to dream was possible. I belonged to someone and soon little ones would belong to me.

Not that I had any idea what to do with them. For all intents and purposes, I was an only child with a mean selfish streak. As much as I reveled in having a family of my own, I mourned my loss of independence and freedom. I felt impatient and easily irritated, lost my temper and yelled, and withheld affection when I felt angry or annoyed, all things I didn't want to do.

Parenting for me was as much a process of maturing myself as it was raising anyone else. Being a mother is like having a magnifying make-up mirror staring you in the face, exposing all your fine lines and wrinkles. All the flaws carefully hidden under the make-up of polite niceties in public are revealed by the Noxzema of parenting small children in private.

Despite my inadequacies as a parent, my babies became my world. My mind went numb watching talking vegetables and animals count to ten and recite the alphabet. I smiled watching them walk around the house in my shoes, stuffing random household items into their toy purses, and pretending to read books they scattered across the floor. Those early days consisted of pearls of laughter chained by strands of tedium.

Many nights I went to bed feeling like a failure. I didn't know how to make them listen or obey me. I didn't know how to make them stop crying and be reasonable. I felt exhausted, bored, and a little bit crazy. I fell to my knees and asked God for wisdom and asked my kids for forgiveness. One of the greatest gifts family members can give each other is modeling how to repent, apologize, and forgive. We've been able to practice a lot, especially since I decided to homeschool.

When they reached the age to start school, I was just starting to have fun with them. They changed from irrational babbling monkeys into interesting little people I wanted to get to know better. No longer consumed by nap schedules, playdates, and tantrum management, we could go on field trips, read books together, and have real conversations. It seemed tragic to me to send them away for hours a day and miss their transformation. My happiest childhood memories were the days I spent with my mom doing things that were special and fun. I wanted to give my daughters as many of those days as I could. Given everything that would happen, I'm glad I did.

CHAPTER 3

The mother who takes pains to endow her children with good habits secures for herself smooth and easy days. – Charlotte Mason

The state of Texas is crawling with giant bugs and home schooling families. Anywhere I went with my baby and toddler (church, the park, McDonalds, etc.), I ran into parents with school age children discussing their educational philosophies and curriculum. I asked a lot of questions, interested in one day joining their ranks. Teaching reading and writing sounded like more fun than the preschool cat herding I was doing at the time. I longed to have real conversations about things besides food and poop and share my passion for history, art, music and literature. I couldn't wait for our adventure to begin.

We moved to Boston a year before our oldest would start Kindergarten and by then I had already decided to homeschool. I'm glad I prepared before we left Texas because when the military moved us to Massachusetts, it felt like immigrating to a different country, one hostile to my kind. I've never lived anywhere so secular, materialistic, and status-driven. Parents obsessed over preparing their preschoolers for Harvard with private tutors, ballet lessons, and $300 finger painting classes.

The drive for achievement and conformity permeated playground conversations. Students could suffocate from the stress of competition. In our Boston suburb, most all of the graduating seniors went to college after graduation, but one year, three committed suicide. I think I'd rather have fewer go to college and none kill themselves because of the stress of meeting unrealistic expectations.

Everyone wants their kids to grow up to be successful adults, but people have different definitions of what success means. Some measure success using investment portfolios, lavish homes, or an Ivy League education. I don't. Anything that glorifies the temporary while ignoring the eternal holds little value to me. An advanced degree is only as impressive as the work the person who holds it does for others. My definition of success rests on doing the good work set before us and being all we were created to be. I want my children to work hard, find their calling, and enjoy their lives, but I refused to join the East Coast obsession with pursuing the highest levels of academia at any costs. Besides, I could buy finger paint for way less than $300.

When making the choice to homeschool, I set myself up to be judged and criticized by people who didn't know me or my family. I became a substitute for all parents who keep their kids at home, for whatever reason. A neighbor brought me a scholarship application to a private preschool program, thinking that lack of money kept me from putting my daughter in school.

Appalled by my decision to keep my daughter out of school, she warned me with a story about some in-laws from California whose relaxed homeschooling resulted in illiterate and unemployable young adults. She worried aloud that though well-meaning, I wasn't a professional. I was taking a risk by keeping them at home. They might fall behind their peers academically or not know how to act in social situations with their peers. My blood started to boil as my neighbor implied that she cared more for my children's education and development than I did. "Kindergarten isn't rocket science. I'm not worried about it," I responded with false confidence.

I was in fact anything but confident. I felt like a boxer that had been smacked around enough to be hurt and dizzy, but not knocked out. I learned to strengthen my defenses by focusing on why I wanted to keep my children home with me. Developing my children's self-confidence, conscience, and critical thinking in the security and safety of our home mattered more to me than fitting in with our neighbors and the culture of our community.

The way my daughter responded to her peers only solidified my resolve to keep her at home. If the older girl who lived next door started to bully a smaller child, my daughter would join her, copying what she said. If I took her to a playdate and her friend was wearing a dress while my daughter had on pants, she would beg to go home and change clothes so she could be the same as her friend. It scared me to see her imitate her friends. I wanted her to feel secure in being herself and doing what she knew to be the right thing, not following someone else's lead. It would be easiest for me to teach her those things if I had more time with her at home.

I also felt confident that I could give her a better academic foundation at home than she would get in school. Not bound by the limitations of a classroom full of students, we could work at our own pace and follow our own interests and moods. Unlike my experience of having to be still and bored for most of the day, my daughter moved, sang, and recited the information she learned. She played school with her little sister, taught her what she learned, and solidified the knowledge in her own mind.

Kindergarten the second time around was a lot more fun than I remembered. We played letter and number games like Memory and Hi Ho Cherry-o. The girls traced letters in trays of sand, finger-painted, and made crafts with Popsicle sticks and cotton balls. Science consisted of experiments using coffee filters, soap, and food coloring. Cardboard and fabric transformed into helmets and swords, castles and boats, costumes and forts. We went to the library and came home with a laundry basket full of books. We marked our calendar with library events and the librarians learned our names.

While the girls looked through their stacks of picture books, I researched different home schooling philosophies. Rather than pick one, I took a little from all of them. For math, I followed a traditional approach using textbooks and workbooks. I used

Charlotte Mason's ideas of using "living books" or narrative writing rather than dry text to teach history. We studied history chronologically like the Classical method and used dictation to practice handwriting and sentence structure. I adopted an eclectic style that may have looked like organized chaos but worked for me.

After a year of going it alone, we joined a homeschool group that gathered once a week for sharing. We met four year olds who wrote short stories and seven year olds able to recite Homer's Iliad. Intimated doesn't begin to describe how I felt. I feared our cardboard Babylonian headdress and Popsicle stick Egyptian boat fell short of the academic excellence that surrounded us. These children of professors, engineers, and doctors far surpassed my standards for early elementary aged kids. They could take the SAT and my kids couldn't even sit still for more than an hour.

Comparing my kids to the ones I saw at the homeschoolers group sent me into a whirlwind of worry. My kids and I didn't do enough, they weren't learning enough. With renewed seriousness, I scheduled daily dictation, math drills, and flash card quizzing until we all felt miserable. Eventually, we went back to what we'd been doing: playing, exploring, and reading in a loosely followed schedule.

I pushed my fears to the back of my mind and focused being more intentional. I adopted the Charlotte Mason philosophy of taking the girls on nature walks and noting observations in a sketchbook. I turned trips to the local parks into opportunities to name the trees and birds we saw. They probably don't remember the names, but they remember the walks.

I'd love to say I raised my kids television free and never used it as a babysitter, but I would be lying. I put kid's television time in the daily schedule after breakfast. I knew the shows at that hour would be age appropriate and I could get housework done while they watched. Sometimes they didn't want to sit and watch, making me a little crazy. I never thought of putting them to work doing chores like my mom did to me and I probably should have. Instead, I helped them stay occupied playing while I cleared the clutter and folded the laundry.

Some days the girls played dolls all morning while I cleaned house. On other days, we sat around watching cartoon videos all day. I was hardly a drill sergeant or the model of discipline. However, I consistently read to them every day and made every effort to get them to read as well. The older one learned by the traditional method of memorizing sight words and letter sounds, sounding out words, and doing phonics exercises. The other seemed to just pick up a book and start reading one day. It was fascinating to watch them both grow in skill and knowledge each day.

I listened to them read, stopped them when they came to an unfamiliar word, and asked them what it meant. If they didn't know, I would have them guess and we would discuss synonyms that could take the word's place. After they finished reading, we would talk about the characters in the narrative, the setting, and the themes addressed in the story or passage. This was the part of homeschooling that I loved.

Homeschooling brought other benefits like bonding as a family and maintaining childhood innocence. Instead of getting the last tired hours of the day, we spent our best hours with each other. My husband and I watched the girls dance around the living room or acted as an audience for impromptu puppet shows. When we watched television or listened to music together and something came on that I didn't like, I explained why I didn't like it and asked them what they thought about it. Soon they became their own police and I didn't have to say anything. If they heard or saw something they knew I wouldn't approve of, they turned it off or changed the channel without prompting.

My goal was to instill my values in them so that when they grew older, they would make decisions on their own that reflected what they'd been taught at home. I knew they would be inundated with the warped values and stereotypes broadcast in media. So, I taught them to guard their hearts and minds. By having them with me, I could monitor their media diet and provide guidance and influence over their choices. I gave them defenses from the attacks of materialism, sexuality, and vanity by arming them with facts.

When we moved back to my hometown in Washington State, I felt less adamant about keeping the girls at home. I felt more comfortable with the more conservative culture and partnership between parents, schools, and community but, we were still having fun doing our thing at home.

Then I learned about a homeschool partnership program offered by our local school district. Students took enrichment classes with other home schooled children two days a week and the district reimbursed parents for the cost of approved curriculum and music lessons. In exchange, parents agreed to draft a learning plan and attend monthly meetings with an advisor teacher to discuss progress and learning goals. It sounded like a good fit for us. The girls could socialize with other kids and I could enjoy a little bit of a break.

I appreciated the forced organization required by the public school program and the guidance and accountability it provided. At the beginning of each year I had a blueprint of learning objectives and a list of tools we would use. The advisor approved the books I used so I continued to choose my own courses of study, regardless of what students in the public school studied at the time.

Because I used a literature-based, history-driven approach, the era of history chosen for the year determined the course content. I used <u>A Child's History of the World</u> as a simple narrative when the girls were little and when we re-visited it later, they vaguely remembered hearing the stories before. From their reading assignments and the books I read aloud, I assigned writing and research projects. I bought workbooks for vocabulary, grammar, reading comprehension, and analogies. We used a standard curriculum for math because math isn't my strong suit and I didn't want to get creative. Our year ran smoothly as the girls completed sections in chronological order.

As the years passed, differences in personality and preferences emerged. One child loved to be with people all the time, the other liked to work alone in her room. The creative writer could spin a yarn long enough to knit a sweater while the voracious reader preferred just the facts. One sister tried to complete her assignments as quickly as possible while the other made her work last the entire day, taking frequent breaks. Both liked to sing at the top of their lungs while doing math work. They competed by singing different songs at the same time. "No singing while doing math!" I frequently yelled. Despite their differences, the girls got along most of the time.

My older daughter wondered what traditional school was like. She worried that because most kids spend seven hours in school and she worked for only three that they must be more advanced or learning more than she was. She also wanted to be with more people. Hours conversing with her mother didn't adequately fulfill her need for social interaction. She asked to try regular public school, just part time to see what it was like. Starting the beginning of 7th grade, she took choir, math, and science at the local middle school and came home in the afternoon to study history and language arts with me. My younger daughter stayed in the cooperative program and we continued to work together three days a week.

We navigated the home school waters with only a few storms until I got sick, but we didn't know I was sick at the time. The girls thought I was making them responsible for more of their work on purpose, to try teach them to be more independent and less lazy.

They figured my asking them the same questions over and over and repeating myself was just me being annoying, making sure they were doing their work. Yet, there was something different about me. I had gone from giving them my full attention to barely phoning it in. Between not wanting to get out of bed in the morning and not remembering what we were doing when I did, I was not the mom they were used to having. They were the first to see the change, but the least able to do something about it. It would take other people noticing for that to happen.

CHAPTER 4

It's a bit like walking down a long, dark corridor
and never knowing when the light will go on.
– Neil Lennon, on depression

I thought my hormones were out of whack for a little while and that the way I was feeling would pass in time. It wasn't unusual for me to feel temporarily depressed. All my life, I've come down with the blues. For a time, life loses its glimmer and goes from color to black and white; nothing seems worth the expense of too much energy. As much as I would want to be around people, it made me feel lonelier, so I kept to myself. Every time this happens, I eventually snap out of it and life returns to normal (or what I consider normal anyway).

I have learned different techniques to deal with it. In college, my coping mechanism was eating a whole pizza alone in my dorm room, watching soap operas. I wrote lengthy letters to entertain friends that lived far away, detailing the dramas of dorm life. When the girls were smaller and the blues struck, I would leave them with their dad and wander the aisles at Target, combing the Clearance racks for treasures. It was my form of retail therapy. I didn't even have to buy anything to feel better. I could just pretend the store was my own personal museum where I went to view my things. During my most recent bout of gloom, I took up running and that seemed to work, until it didn't anymore.

I tried to organize, motivate, and will myself into normalcy but, I couldn't shake the feeling that I was falling apart. The competent, capable woman I thought I was had been replaced by a tired, depressed woman who had trouble sleeping, organizing her thoughts, or getting tasks completed. I started waking in the middle of the night. A confusing conversation would play like a broken record in my mind or anxiety would wash over me like a tidal wave, making me feel like I was drowning, unable to get enough air. I would jolt awake with my heart racing and not be able to fall back asleep. I read or made lists of things to do when it was really time to get up. Sometimes I would doze off a few minutes before the alarm would ring to wake me up for good.

After silencing the alarm, I would lie on my back and pray. "Oh God, help me get everything done today. Give me the right attitude to do my work without feeling like a hopeless mess," I pleaded. I pondered a mental to do list for my personal assistant. Then, lacking such a luxury, I would get up and do those things myself. I struggled to get out of bed every day and go about the business of running a household, raising kids, and fulfilling my commitments.

People sometimes ask me how long I felt unwell. That's a hard question to answer because my symptoms didn't strike all at once. The melancholy drifted in like a hazy fog, gradually lifting higher and thicker until I was completely surrounded and couldn't see in front of me. It took weeks for me to realize it wasn't the ordinary bout of gloom that would go away on its own.

When friends casually asked, "How are you?" I told them the truth. "I'm not doing so great. I have a mental cold. It might be seasonal. This winter has really been rough on me." This small admission of weakness brought on a slew of well-meaning advice. Keep a gratitude journal. Take Vitamin D. Use a happy light. Try yoga.

Then the questions started. "Have you been running?" or "Have you prayed about it?" It took all I had not to try to turn the questioning around on them. "What's your exercise routine like?" "How's your quiet time with God?" I hated the implied criticism. I prayed and it seemed like no one was listening or answering. Looking back on it now, God was probably yelling, "Go to the doctor!" but it took a while for me to get the message.

Despite feeling judged, I tried to follow the advice and suggestions people gave me. I tried little tweaks to my diet to add more nutrition and reduce calories. I choked down spinach smoothies and horse pill vitamins. I drank watered down cranberry juice instead of soda pop. I ate less bread, started eating open face sandwiches, and tried unfamiliar grains and vegetables. I choked down as much green stuff as I could, even though it tasted like grass clippings. (I don't care what anyone says, kale is disgusting. In a chip, in a smoothie, or in a salad, it's just gross.)

I drank herbal tea and sports drinks with potassium. I took Melatonin at night and sat next to a 'happy light'. The Melatonin actually worked but my cat enjoyed the light more than I did. It just gave me headaches. I kept a gratitude journal, went to exercise classes, and listened to classical music. I did everything I knew to do, except see a doctor. Nothing I did made me feel better.

Christmas came and went. I couldn't face the prospect of taking down the decorations. The season hovered like a dark storm cloud. Through the parties, the concerts, the baking, and the presents, it seemed like my world stayed dark. I waited for a ray of sunshine to break through but, I couldn't get into the holiday spirit. The decorations stayed in place through January until I finally got tired of looking at them and took them down.

Not only did I feel sad, but I felt guilty for feeling sad. I knew in my heart that my life was full of blessings and I should be feeling joy and gratitude. I had a comfortable home, a healthy family, and a supportive spouse. My needs were met and I lived in a pleasant community. I wanted to feel happy but instead I felt meaningless. I knew I mattered to my husband and my kids, but I felt pointless to the rest of the world. My world seemed small and insignificant.

King Solomon wrote in the books of Ecclesiastes, "As I

looked at everything I had worked so hard to accomplish, it was all so meaningless. It was like chasing the wind. There was nothing really worthwhile anywhere." (Ecc. 2:11). That's how I felt, like I was spinning in a hamster wheel going nowhere. My life amounted to an endless cycle of cleaning dishes, doing laundry, and driving kids around town. As much as I wanted to feel happy, the feeling eluded me.

I learned why suffering people often withdraw from relationships and stop interacting with their friends, only making their situation worse. Though I needed to maintain connection with my friends and family to be healthy, it hurt. Like a torn scab, I felt tender and vulnerable. I wanted someone to give me a hug, to keep me company and tell me jokes, not make me feel like Humpty-Dumpty. I didn't want to be put back together again.

I've never been very good at being helpless. If my history taught me anything it was to suck it up and drive on. Don't waste time throwing yourself a pity party. Don't expect sympathy or special treatment. Be responsible and take care of yourself, because no one else will. I was on my own. I didn't want to need anyone because people let me down.

I found the easiest way to cope with difficult situations was to turn off my emotions and use logic and reason to problem solve. I plotted courses of action, played out scenarios in my mind, and made contingency plans. I researched options and weighed pros and cons. I didn't take risks with my safety, health, or finances. I didn't smoke, never got drunk, and avoided being in debt. I married a dependable man with a steady income and I went to church every time the doors were open. I kept my life simple and avoided stressful situations as much as possible. I thought that keeping myself safe made me good and that by being good I could avoid discomfort.

As much as I would like for the world to follow the rules of cause and effect, sometimes bad things happen for no good reason. Sometimes people get sick or depressed and it isn't because they didn't exercise enough or they ate the wrong food. There is no one to blame, no cause to be found. The rain falls on the righteous and the wicked alike and some problems have no easy solutions. That is why people like me, detached problem solvers, are the worst kind of friends of the sick and depressed.

The Bible teaches repeatedly that we are to love one another, to have compassion, and bear each other's burdens. We are to regard others as better than ourselves, considering their needs ahead of our own. Jesus laid down his life for his friends and I'm called to follow his example. Somehow I heard those words but the message that stuck was, "Follow the rules." Do the right thing and be safe.

Even though the Bible never said anything about avoiding pain, that's what I sought to do. I claimed to be a Christian but refused to love like Christ. I clung to my pride, fears, and independence instead of empathizing with the hurting and broken.

Trying to keep my world safe and small and my heart protected from pain prevented me from experiencing the connection I desired.

I learned that I have to be willing to let others in, even when it hurts my ego and pride. I also have to let go of my tendency to want to fix people and situations. When someone is hurting, they don't want to be fixed or given a solution. They want to be loved, accepted, and heard. At least that's what I wanted at the time. When someone tells me about a problem, instead of mentally scrambling for a solution, I need to listen. I want to be the one to say, "You're alright. I'm here for you, whatever you decide to do." Empathy doesn't come naturally to me so I know God is working on me.

Fortunately, I have a few friends that model this kind of empathy. One lived in Massachusetts and had experience with clinical depression. She and I wrote letters back and forth, but one day I decided to call rather than write. After listening to me a short time, she knew I wasn't myself.

"You need to go to the doctor," she said. I told her it wasn't that bad. "Go before it gets that bad. I wish I would have gone sooner," she cajoled, but I didn't listen. God often speaks to me through friends, but usually it takes the same message from multiple sources before He gets through my thick skull. It took some time for the message to get through; I had to completely lose my mind first.

CHAPTER 5

How can I be sure I've succeeded if I can't remember what I was trying to do? –Ashleigh Brilliant

My older daughter, Lauren, came home from her morning classes and asked what I wanted her to do. I sighed and gave her the answer I gave every day, "Do whatever is next in your book."

"What book?" she replied. I taught using literature books I assigned her to read, a Latin roots vocabulary workbook, and a history textbook. I made up questions and writing assignments at the end of the chapters. The answer 'whatever is next in your book' wasn't enough. After finishing her assigned literature book and finishing her Latin, she didn't know what to do next. The daily questioning drove me crazy because I didn't know how to answer. I felt like I was losing my mind.

I had a general idea of what concepts and themes of history I wanted her to glean from her reading and writing assignments, but I didn't have a structured schedule with an assignment list. I struggled to keep track of what she had already finished and what would come next. With more time and less anxiety, I could have reviewed my outlines and book selections and assigned her essay questions. Instead, I wracked my brain trying to remember what I had planned months ago.

In frustration, I grabbed a biography of a founding father off the shelf and asked, "Have you read this one yet? No? Well, here you go. Start reading. Then write a book report."

"What do you mean by book report?" she wanted to know.

"What do you mean, what do I mean? I'm not speaking a foreign language. Write me a book report."

"What do you want me to write?"

"I can't tell you that. I didn't read the book. Just give a summary of what you read and what you learned from it."

"How long does it have to be?"

"Long enough to cover the information."

"How long is that? A paragraph? A page? What do you want?"

"I want you to stop bugging me and read your stupid book!"

"If it's stupid, why do I have to read it?"

"YOU'RE DRIVING ME INSANE. GO AWAY!"

Once she finished her reading, she continued to ask for

clarification or help. I couldn't remember what I had or hadn't told her to do and the constant badgering made me frustrated and angry, which in turn, made her frustrated and angry. We acted like combatants and everyday brought a new battle. This wasn't how I intended homeschooling to go. We had some healthy debates in the past but nothing like this, leaving us both feeling frustrated and confused. And it happened every day.

Carolyn, our younger daughter, went to school two days a week so we crammed five days' worth of work into three. I tried to get her to do most of it on Tuesday and Thursday so I didn't nag or badger her on a busy Friday, when I taught at a community homeschool cooperative and did my grocery shopping. Her laid back pace obliterated my hopes of having a shortened day. I indulged her tendency to ask "Can I have a 15 minute break?" every 15 minutes on days I wasn't pressed for time and it came back to bite me on days when I was.

"Come sit with my while I do my math so you can help me if I get stuck," she requested.

"I'll work through the first couple problems with you but then you are on your own," I replied.

Between moving laundry from washer to dryer, unloading the dishwasher, and preparing for grocery shopping, I couldn't sit at the table with her and walk her through every assignment. All she had to do was finish her assignments for the day. I had an entire house to clean, a week of meals to plan and prepare, and a list of errands that I had to run. I needed her to work independently so I could get my work done.

I knew that teaching my daughter was more important than cleaning the house but I couldn't stop feeling undone. I sat with her at the table and watched her work. Then, a thought popped into my head of something that needed to be done and I felt like I had to do it immediately or I might forget. Urgent tasks divided my attention and without supervision, my daughter felt discouraged and unimportant.

Our home life was falling apart. I felt defeated and incapable of teaching the way I wanted my kids to be taught. We were supposed to be making happy childhood memories, not fighting about responsibility and unmet expectations. I don't know if I had done too much for them in the past or was doing too little for them in the present, but what we were doing wasn't working for any of us. Whatever was happening with me was going beyond a season of depression.

One morning, I woke up and I couldn't remember what day it was. My mind was like an Etch-A-Sketch someone kept shaking when I wasn't paying attention. I had a list of things to do in my head but couldn't figure out if and when they needed to be done, or if I had done them already. Paranoia settled over me as I realized how bad my short-term memory had become. I had always had an excellent memory and knew this was not normal for me, but I figured this was just another symptom of the depression I had been struggling with for so long.

At first, I played detective to find out what I was forgetting by looking at the calendar or to-do lists I left laying on my desk, but then my schedule became more chaotic and my to-do lists started to overwhelm me. I started to forget things people told me, right after they told me. I would get off the phone with someone, remember who was on the phone, but completely forget what was said. I found myself asking the same question over and over until I wrote down the answer and could look at the paper to remember.

I wrote notes to myself. I felt like the main character in the movie *Memento* who suffered from memory loss so severe he started tattooing information on his body. I wasn't THAT bad, but I could see how that technique could be useful. What was worse than jotting down notes all the time was that the words wouldn't mean anything to me because I couldn't remember writing them.

Each morning I laid in bed trying to remember what happened the day before to see if I could figure out what day it was. Once I figured that out, I had to remember where everyone was going on that particular day and at what time. Carolyn went to classes at the local elementary school two days each week, Mondays and Wednesdays. She got picked up in the afternoon at the YMCA. Lauren went to the middle school every morning at 8:00am and got picked up at 10:51am unless it was Wednesday. Wednesdays she had to be picked up at 10:21am.

Every day when I dropped her off, I would ask her when she needed to be picked up and she would roll her eyes, as middle-school aged children do, and say, "Same time as yesterday." To which I would reply, "And what time is that?" Not realizing why I couldn't remember even the most basic information, my questions confused and annoyed my kids.

I had Monday and Wednesday mornings to myself to plan our homeschooling, go for a walk with a friend, or go out to breakfast. I liked that little break in my routine but it started to bother me when I couldn't remember where the girls were and what time I was supposed to pick them up. If I was with a friend, I'd ask her to remind me of the time so I wouldn't forget. I usually didn't, but I was afraid that I would.

It was especially bad if there was any modification to my regular schedule. I couldn't remember what I was told or what I had agreed to do. I wished I could have the exact same routine every day so I could just be on auto-pilot, but that couldn't happen. My calendar was full of once a month, once a week, or random meeting dates.

For example, one week a month, Lauren had group lesson instead of individual lesson for piano and group was at a different time. If I remembered to take her to group, then I would forget to take her to her lesson the following week because my routine had been changed. Our 4-H group met once a month and I would wonder every week, is this the week I'm supposed to lead our 4-H club?

I scheduled appointments with some of the girls in our club to come over and sew at my house. Even though most of them had very simple projects of elastic waist skirts or pajama bottoms, items I could sew in my sleep, I agonized over getting them done. Twice, I forgot I had someone coming, left home to go somewhere else, and had to reschedule. Fretting that they wouldn't finish and I would be to blame, I turned simple sewing projects into behemoth challenges. I was losing confidence in myself and felt like an old woman with dementia.

If I did keep the appointment, we would get a lot accomplished in sewing but not without me asking over and over, "Where did (fill in the tool here) go?" It was typical for me to misplace scissors, pins, or seam rippers when my memory was intact. It was much worse when it wasn't. One mother told me that I complimented her daughter's fabric many times and asked her where she got it more than once.

I was constantly apologizing to everyone for my disorganization, telling them I was out of sorts. I wouldn't know until later how concerned others were about my mental state. I was not the calm, confident instructor they were used to seeing. Everyone knew there was something wrong with me but they didn't say anything to me about it. They weren't used to seeing me so frustrated and disorganized but didn't make a big deal about it. If only they had!

There were times I had volunteer obligations spinning in my head and I wasn't sure if I had agreed to do them or not. The county 4-H program hosted a day of classes one Saturday in March. I remembered attending a planning meeting, brainstorming class subject ideas, and suggesting possible instructors. I couldn't remember if I had volunteered myself or not. By this time, I knew I was in no shape to teach anything, but I didn't want to be a flake.

I called to see what I had volunteered myself to do and was reassured that I was not teaching anything but was going to help police the halls to make sure all the kids were in their assigned classes. I told the coordinator that I wasn't well, and she assured me that my absence would not be a huge inconvenience. They had plenty of volunteers to cover the policing duties. Even with the reassurance, I couldn't help but think I was letting people down because of my inability to remember what I was supposed to be doing.

My short-term memory loss impacted my two daughters long before anyone else realized anything was seriously wrong with me. Because we homeschooled, they spent more time with me than anyone else and depended on me to be organized and structured. I was failing them because I couldn't remember what they were learning. My mind remembered with clarity why I started this journey, but could not recall where we were. It's hard to reach your destination when you are lost and unable to remember the directions.

As much as I loved being home with my kids, choosing what

they learned, and teaching them how to think for themselves, I needed help. In order to be involved, but not fully responsible, switching to full-time school seemed like a good option. On February 15th, our younger daughter Carolyn started 4th grade at public school. Lauren didn't want to make the leap into full-time public school in the middle of the year so she decided to continue as a part-time student and work more independently at home.

I had valid reasons for homeschooling. Schools can be a dangerous place for tender hearts and minds, full of bullies and bad influences. Up to this point, I didn't have to worry about these things. Now I would. I had given my kids the security and connection I missed as a child, but I couldn't do it through homeschooling anymore. What had been the right choice for our family had become an untenable one. The life we had was coming to an end and I had to surrender control and see what would happen.

Through this transition, God gave me peace about leaving homeschooling. He showed me that He was in control of our homeschooling the whole time, not me. By His grace, I had the health, the ability, and the wherewithal to educate my children at home. If He hadn't been working in me, I couldn't have done it because I'm not naturally a kid person. I had no idea what I was doing when my children were born and yet God blessed me with the opportunity to model and guide them to a personal relationship with Him. Homeschooling had been a gift to me.

God's sovereignty didn't end at our front door. He faithfully stayed with my kids even when I was away from them, just as He stayed with me throughout my history. With all the chaos in my mind, I didn't worry about them when they weren't with me. Unfortunately, I still had to remember when they needed to be picked up. It wasn't easy and it got harder every day.

CHAPTER 6

*To what will you look for help if you will not
look to that which is stronger than yourself?*
— C.S. Lewis, Mere Christianity

The second weekend in March, a friend invited me to travel
with her to a baby shower for a mutual friend that had moved to
Seattle. Before we even left town, I contacted her three or four times
to confirm when we were leaving and when we needed to arrive. I
couldn't remember if we had set a time or not and I wanted to make
sure we had enough time to arrive before the party.

I thought that maybe I could pass as normal as long as I
didn't talk about our plans for the weekend. Instead, we talked about
our college days, how we met our husbands, and our relationships
with extended family. As my long-term memory was unaffected, I
could talk about my past and ask questions without seeming
completely lost. I thought, "So far, so good. Maybe I can get
through the weekend without looking like an idiot."

Unfortunately, without the structure and familiarity of my
home and schedule, I was lost. I tried to remind myself to be easy

going but, that's not easy for me. I've never been very good at letting others lead without knowing where they were leading. I didn't know what time we were having dinner or what time we were leaving for home and I would ask over and over again, sometimes consciously, sometimes not. As much as I tried, I could not hold on to any new information.

After I went to bed, my friends stayed awake talking about how there must be something wrong with me. My behavior had them very worried. In the morning they told me, "You need to see a naturopath as soon as you get home and we will make an appointment for you."

I smiled without protest or argument. Inside, I was putting up a fight. I thought to myself, "Give me a break. I'm not going to some hippie nature freak that's going to tell me take some tree bark extract or give up gluten and dairy." As much as I respected my friends' concern, I didn't share their faith in alternative medicine. I knew they were right about needing to see someone; I just wasn't willing to go see a naturopath. If what I had could be cured without going to a doctor, it probably wasn't that bad.

As much as I tried to pretend it wasn't, my condition worsened by the day. Along with the memory loss, periodic headaches went from dull to painful. At first, I thought it was from trying a "happy light" a friend let me borrow, but they didn't go away even after I gave up on the light. After months of being clean and sober from Mountain Dew, I fell off the wagon and started drinking again because it gave me relief from the headaches. I didn't want to go back to the old days of feeling like I needed the shot of sugar and caffeine I got from drinking soda pop every day, but it was the only thing that took the pain away.

Before the headaches and memory loss, I had signed up to chaperone a school trip to see the Broadway show, West Side Story, in Kennewick, a 50 mile drive from our home in Walla Walla. I didn't feel like going, but it was a special event and I couldn't back out at the last minute. We left in the afternoon and returned late that evening. I nodded off a couple times during the show and didn't remember hearing any of my favorite songs. I asked Lauren about it and she sighed and rolled her eyes. "Yes Mom, they sang *I Feel Pretty* and *America*. You just weren't paying attention."

"I was paying attention. I just don't remember."

"Try not falling asleep," she sarcastically suggested.

"Yeah, I'll try that," I said, wishing I didn't have to try so hard.

At home, my husband Ben had come down with a nasty cold that had taken a turn for the worse. Ben had life-threatening pneumonia when he was stationed in Korea in the Army and because of it, a weakened respiratory system. The cold went into his chest, making it hard for him to breathe. He called a family friend who is also a doctor and he recommended that Ben go to the emergency room. He and his wife met Ben at the hospital and stayed with him until he was released. He was home when we returned from the trip, but still miserable.

The next day, I tried to play nurse the best I could, but I wasn't very good at it. Fluffing pillows, bringing medicine and water, and running to the store for soup and crackers proved almost too much for me. It was hard enough dropping off and picking up the girls at the right times, trying to prepare for a meeting for work, and keeping the house straight. I buzzed around from room to room, forgetting what I'd done and what I still needed to do.

I worked as the secretary for a physicians' organization and I had to attend one of their dinner meetings. I went, leaving Ben sick at home with the girls. I tried my best to act normal, but apparently I told the neurologist with whom I sat that I needed to come see him because I was losing my mind. He told me that he was retired but I should probably go see my family doctor. The interaction is a blur, but he told me later he will never forget the conversation we had. I do remember sitting next to him at dinner. It makes sense to me that I would tell the brain doctor that my brain wasn't working.

The wife of the doctor that helped Ben was at the meeting and noticed that I seemed out of sorts. I was forgetful and disorganized and that made her suspicious that something was physiologically wrong with me. She called and talked to me on the phone the next day. She gathered enough information from our conversation to determine that I needed to be seen by a physician and scheduled me an appointment. Ben also had an appointment so she went with me to mine. I thought that she convinced the doctor to order an MRI but she later insisted that it didn't take much convincing. A short conversation with me was sufficient. The nurse asked me what month it was, I said January. It was March.

On Friday, the test was ordered, performed, and a follow-up appointment scheduled. Ben was well enough to attend the Monday follow-up appointment with me. We waited anxiously for the doctor to give us the results. He came in, sat down, and leaned in. He spoke in a very matter of fact sort of way with a neutral expression. He told us the MRI showed a mass the size of a quarter in the center of my brain and let us look at the image. The mass consisted of a small hard tumor part and a liquid cyst part. With the cyst, it measured three centimeters. It looked like a golf ball in the center of my brain, sitting in a little space between my frontal lobe, my optic nerve, and my pituitary gland.

He said my case presented in an unusual way. This kind of tumor is usually diagnosed in children or found with other symptoms like vision changes or hormonal issues. The cyst looked like it was putting pressure on the optic nerve and the back of my frontal lobe, the personality part of the brain. It wasn't clear why I was losing my memory. It was possible that removing the tumor would clear my memory issues or maybe not.

I understood what he was saying, but I didn't know how to respond or feel about it. It was as though he was describing the condition of someone else and I was pondering what it would be like to be that person. It was like I was watching two people talk to their doctor on a television show. It didn't feel like he was talking about me. It was surreal.

I recall him saying something about Gamma ray knives. It sounded like something out of a Star Trek movie. They use radiation like a tiny laser beam to zap the tumor and make it die. A brace holds the patient perfectly still and no actual cutting is required. That ray gun thingy sounded good because I couldn't imagine having my head cut open, someone moving my brains around, and then stitching me back up like Frankenstein's monster. It was too much to imagine.

He made it clear that this was not his area of expertise and that he would transfer us to a specialist right away. Only then could we get our questions answered. The doctor referred us to a neurosurgeon in Portland and we were on our way to find out how I could get my brain back.

Ben and I walked like zombies out of the doctor's office. Feeling weak and congested, he grappled with the diagnosis. The old wife he had trusted with all his household and financial logistics was gone and replaced by a new wife who couldn't be trusted to answer the telephone. He didn't know if he would ever get the old wife back and was scared to death of this new one.

And I knew it. I was scared for him. I wasn't sure he could handle all of his responsibilities and take on mine as well. It would be a multi-tasking nightmare for a man who liked to focus on one thing at a time. Ben had always been a man of many talents, but handling stressful situations was not one of them. That was my job.

Anxiety overwhelmed me. I wanted the world to see me as smart, capable, and responsible. For anyone to think I was incompetent or careless broke my heart and wounded my ego. I wrapped my identity in my ability to lead, organize, and get things done. My confidence in myself evaporated and all that remained was the fear that I had become a worthless liability instead of a valuable asset. In the past, there had been times when I trusted others to take care of me and they disappointed me. I turned that disappointment into armor of self-sufficiency. It had served me well for many years, but now it was worthless.

In this place of utter weakness and despair, God showed me that my armor of self-sufficiency could not be worn at the same time as His armor. I had to take off my breastplate of self-righteousness if I wanted to wear His righteousness, which doesn't depend on my ability to be good at everything. I had to remove my helmet of self-help and remember that my help comes from the maker of heaven and earth. Remembering God's provision and grace would be my helmet of salvation. Instead of blistering my spiritual feet with anxiousness, I needed to lace up the sandals of peace, resting in the knowledge that my value comes not from what I do, but what God does for me. I had to take off my pride so I could rest in grace.

Tullian Tchividijian wrote, "Preoccupation with my effort

over God's effort for me makes me increasingly self-centered and morbidly introspective." Morbidly introspective is a fancy way of saying depressed and preoccupation with my effort describes precisely what I was doing, focusing on my ability to fix myself instead of believing God's promises for my life. I came to the realization that I needed to think less about myself and my performance and more about Jesus and His performance for me. I was trusting God. At this point, it seemed like the only logical thing to do.

CHAPTER 7

Yes, there are many parts, but only one body.
The eye can never say to the hand, "I don't need
you." The head can't say to the feet, "I don't
need you." – I Corinthians 12:20-21

Still in shock from the diagnosis, Ben did everything in his power to find someone with a zapper that could bring his wife back from the land of dementia. After making a few phone calls to our insurance company, he discovered that our doctor had accidentally referred us to a medical group out of our insurance network. Instead of traveling to Portland, I needed to be seen at the University of Washington Medical Center in Seattle. We looked forward with dread to a longer drive over a mountain pass and a delay in getting an appointment because the scheduling process had to start from scratch.

On the Wednesday before Easter, our doctor's office told Ben that he would get a call from Seattle soon telling him my appointment time. Ben wanted to be in Seattle as soon as possible so that we could get to the doctor's office at the earliest available appointment. It was important to him to hit the road so we were on

our way or in Seattle when we received the call from the doctor's
office.

We made some phone calls and made arrangements for our
girls to stay with Lauren's best friend's family. The girls didn't mind
being left behind. They loved the family hosting them and they hated
long car rides, especially if there was nothing fun planned for them at
the final destination. They also knew we were unsure when we
would be home and they didn't want to miss school and other
activities. Spring was a busy time of year for the kids. Lauren had a
track meet and Carolyn had a talent show performance. Our friends
graciously recorded her song so we could watch it when we returned.
It was kind of them to take the girls on short notice without knowing
when we would return, but they didn't hesitate to help us.

Even though my mind wasn't working right, I remember a lot
of what happened. I just remember it in an abstract sort of way, like a
painting with splotchy figures and bright colors of emotion. It was
like being in a realistic dream, the kind that makes your heart race or
your temples sweat. I couldn't remember the words people said, but
I distinctly remember who I was with and how they were feeling at
the time.

Before this experience, I struggled to be able to read people.
I had difficulty knowing what others were feeling and frequently
overanalyzed conversations looking for clues. I could remember
word for word what was said, but often missed the nonverbal
communication. Now, I was like an emotionally deaf person who

received new hearing aids. In tune to other's feeling, the emotional noise filled my head. Like a sponge, I soaked up every sigh, eye roll, and frown, but I lost the words that went with them.

Even though I couldn't remember what people told me in the present, I could recall the past with haunting clarity, full of sound and fury. My past memories of traveling in the city with my husband were mostly fury. A man of the open road, he despised traffic. I dreaded navigating the crowded streets of Seattle with him. His own illness and the fear of losing me left Ben sorely unable to deal with the stress of our situation. His stress became my stress.

I called my best friend (I'll call her BFF) and she offered to take us to Seattle so we didn't have to worry about navigating through the city. I explained to Ben that her cousin in the east suburb of Kirkland offered to let us stay at her home so we wouldn't have to get a hotel and he reluctantly agreed to have BFF drive.

Wednesday evening, we walked into the cousin's house to find it in the middle of a major kitchen remodel. The contents of every drawer and cupboard sat in boxes throughout the living room and dining area. The floor boards had holes where appliances used to be and lines where new cupboards were to be installed. Those cupboards sat in cardboard boxes at the end of the room. It was a full blown construction site. Ben wanted to leave, but we had nowhere to go and no car to take us anywhere.

I was just happy we had a construction free bedroom and a

comfortable bed to sleep in. I ignored the mess because it seemed like that's what the people who lived there were doing. We probably wouldn't have opened our home to guests while remodeling, but I'm glad they did.

The doctor's office didn't call during our drive to Seattle and they hadn't called after we arrived. I asked Ben over and over if I had an appointment yet and he said not to worry about it, that he would take care of it. I was not satisfied with that answer. I wanted to know exactly what he had done and what his plan was. He probably told me. I don't remember. He patiently answered me, as though I only asked once. Then I panicked. I couldn't find my purse. I thought I had it with me, but I couldn't find it anywhere. I asked Ben if he knew where my purse was.

"I left it on our dresser at home," he nonchalantly responded. A few minutes later, I forgot his answer and asked him again. Same answer.

My blood started to boil. I couldn't believe he would do such a thing. My unconscious daily habits acted as the safety rope attaching me to reality and keeping me from falling into the abyss of forgetfulness. Having my purse was one of those precious habits. I felt lost without it.

Ben feared I would accidently forget it somewhere and not remember where, which may have happened once or twice when my memory still worked. He didn't want the stress the possibility of losing my credit cards and everything else I carry with me would create. Logically, it made sense, but he might as well have chopped off my arm and left it on the dresser at home.

"WHAT? What about my wallet with my Driver's License and Insurance Card?"

"I took those out and put them in my wallet. I didn't want you to worry about leaving your purse somewhere, so I left it at home."

"That was a <u>BAD</u> idea. Where's my cell phone?"

"I have that too."

"What happens if we go to the city and you lose me? I have no identification, no money, and no phone. What if I forget where I am or who I am? Here I am, a defenseless woman with a brain tumor who can't remember anything. It's stupid to send me out into the world with nothing that tells who I am!" I ranted with a little sarcasm. Up to that point, I had never forgotten who I was.

"We aren't going to lose you. Don't worry about it."

"STOP TELLING ME NOT TO WORRY. IT'S DRIVING ME CRAZY....LIKE NOT HAVING MY PURSE!"

The next day, BFF drove us into the city to visit my brother who lives downtown. I was still irritated about not having my purse and Ben was irritated about not getting a phone call from the clinic.

Then, BFF suggested he call and talk to someone at the clinic. She said something about how her dad (who is the kind of guy who gets things done, if you know what I mean) would go to the hospital, make a scene, and not leave until a doctor saw his wife. Poor Ben felt like the women were ganging up on him when the clinic finally called giving us an appointment time of 1 pm on Monday.

"Monday? What day is it today?" I asked.

"Today is Thursday," Ben answered, in the kindest tone his stressed state would allow.

"Why did we come to Seattle on Wednesday, if we aren't seeing a doctor until Monday?"

"We didn't know the appointment wouldn't be until Monday. We thought we'd be seen this week. It didn't work out."

"We shouldn't have left home until we had an appointment time," said the all-wise woman with the brain tumor.

"It's too late now," he replied in an irritated tone.

"Oh good. We can go home and come back," thought BFF, not wanting to miss the Easter holiday with her family.

That seemed like pure craziness to Ben and me. Why would we spend an extra ten hours in a car and drive 650 miles to come back in three days? BFF hadn't planned on being away all weekend. Ben didn't say much, but was very upset because we were dependent on her for our housing and transportation.

My brother and his wife tried to ease the tension between the three of us by taking us to the waterfront. We rode on the Ferris wheel that overlooks the Puget Sound and walked through Pike Place Market. The uneasy peace dissipated on our walk to get dinner.

My cell phone rang and Ben answered it. It was Lauren, breathless and upset about the results of her track meet. She wanted to talk to me so Ben handed me the phone. BFF didn't think I should be the one calming Lauren, given that I was a mental case that couldn't remember what day it was. She told Ben he should handle calls from home himself and not pass them on to me. That was the last straw for Ben.

As I counseled Lauren over the phone, Ben tried to get away before he completely lost it. BFF followed him. He pushed her and yelled at her to leave him alone. As I got off the phone, I tried to go after Ben, but everyone said to let him go. I couldn't figure out why he flipped out so suddenly. I thought it was because he was unhappy about what we were going to have for dinner. No one would tell me what happened and I felt sick to my stomach. BFF was noticeably shaken. She wasn't used to seeing my usually mild-mannered Ben act this way.

We met back up at the apartment, Ben apologized for the way he acted and we drove back to Kirkland. The drive across Lake Washington was quiet and tense. Ben sat silently in the back as I quizzed BFF about what was going to happen. I didn't know what had happened between the two of them. All I knew is that BFF wanted to go home for Easter and we wanted to stay in Seattle.

I figured we'd just stay put for the weekend and wait for BFF to come back on Sunday night. Ben didn't want to stay at the construction site with strangers for the weekend so he called my friend, Opera Girl, who lived across the Puget Sound from Seattle on the peninsula. Even though we hadn't seen her in ages, she agreed to come get us. She talked to BFF and between the two of them, they worked out a plan to get us to my doctor's appointment on Monday and back home again.

Opera Girl, who I met while singing in our college choir, offered to pick us up and take us to her beach house, drive us to the doctor's appointment on Monday, and meet BFF half way between Seattle and Walla Walla to get us home. I felt overwhelmed with gratitude by her offer to come to our rescue. Even though we barely kept in touch, she acted like no time had passed since I spent Christmas vacation with her family years ago.

Having talked to both Ben and BFF, OG knew we were wrecked and did everything in her power to put us at ease. It was an impossible task. We couldn't tell her what we wanted to eat or where we wanted to go. We were like indecisive, unhappy children. Without any certainty or control, Ben found being dependent on my free-spirited friends torturous. He longed for his own car and a hotel room with no people in it but us.

The beach house offered the most beautiful views of the Hood Canal that you could possibly imagine, but the house itself was a run-down hospice where bad furniture went to die. Worn plaid couches filled the downstairs living area and old mattresses filled the upstairs. It was a blind man's worst nightmare, a maze of large, solid objects.

The temperature dropped to near freezing and we snuggled under multiple blankets to stay toasty in the far back corner of the sleeping area. I passed out but Ben woke up in the middle of the night, dripping in sweat. His heart raced and he couldn't see anything in the black night. "Help! I can't see anything! I need a light!"

OG jumped out of her bed in the next room and brought him a flash light. His chest still pounding, he sounded out of breath, like he had been running in a sprinting contest. She led him downstairs and made him some hot chocolate. Meanwhile, I slept like a dead person, completely unaware of all the middle of the night action.

The next morning, while Ben felt a triple dose of stress from still feeling sick, not having his car, and not knowing what was going to happen to me, my biggest stress was remembering where I set my soda pop and trying to find it again. Opera Girl said I opened five or six cans and left them all over the house, accusing her or Ben of moving them or drinking them when I found them empty. I guess I thought they were trying to ration me or something. No one dared to get between me and the Dew.

Even though I said and did crazy stuff, like accusing my friend of stealing my drinks, in many ways, I felt normal. OG and I sang together, talked about our extended families, and reminisced about college days. We discussed having my family come in the summer and go out on the water. I offered to come and help her clear the cupboards of all the pots and pans that had come to die along with the couches. As long as the discussion focused on the future or the past, things registered. If it had to do with the present or near future, it went in one ear and out the other.

That afternoon, Ben got his wish for us to have time alone. OG had stopped by the store with us and bought food we liked and a case of my beloved Mountain Dew, knowing she was leaving for the city. She had plans to visit friends and perform in an Easter concert. I was confused because I kept forgetting that she told me that she was leaving us alone at the beach. She said goodbye and promised to return on Sunday afternoon.

The beach house felt like a well-stocked deserted island, isolated miles from civilization, which it was. Our weekend could have been relaxing if I hadn't spent Saturday night and Sunday morning asking Ben, "What day is it? When is OG coming back? When is my doctor's appointment again? Where is my Mountain Dew?"

Ben struggled to process everything that was happening. Sickness compromised his health and the possibility of losing me or important parts of my personality plagued his mind. He had never been so frightened in his life. White as a ghost with bags under his eyes, he looked broken and tired. He just wanted to know that I was going to be okay and so far, no one had given that assurance.

We walked along the rocky shore, littered with broken shells and drift wood, holding hands and trying to give each other comfort. We discussed how our actions, words, and tone made each other feel and how we could weather this storm without losing each other. Our talk turned to a discussion about what made us feel secure and loved.

He told me that he felt loved when I used words to express admiration, appreciation, or affection. He needed more of that. I told him that I felt loved when he did things for me. He said he liked to do things for me, but didn't know what I wanted him to do. "That's easy, honey. Just do what I tell you to do!" He told me that he just wanted to take care of me and the girls. He didn't like having my friends or other people so closely involved.

When Ben said that, I felt my face get red and warm. My stomach turned in circles. I knew what he was feeling because I felt it too. Like a beached fish, our pride and self-sufficiency laid dying a slow and painful death on the beach. We needed help.

As much as this crisis could grow us as a couple and a family, it had the potential to tear us apart. I tried in my feeble, flustered way to explain that I didn't want him to take care of me and the girls by himself. I wanted reinforcements because I feared not for my survival, but his. I knew from life experience he would need, we all would need, all the support we could get. We would have to be willing to ask for and accept help, even if it made us feel weak and helpless, which is the worst feeling in the world. We had to get over it and let our independence go.

Ben had a charmed childhood, relatively free of stress and adult responsibilities. He never had to make a meal or do his own laundry. (Thankfully, the army taught him how to do that.) His parents didn't get sick, die, or get divorced. They didn't treat him like a therapist and share their personal problems. They didn't make him pay any bills or tell him that they were too poor for fun. In short, they let him stay a child the entire time he lived with them.

He didn't have any experience with severe stress until he got out on his own. He never got a chance to get good at it like I did. As much as I lament not being taught social skills and being left alone too much, my parents gave me a lot of experience with stressful situations. I lived like an emotional paramedic, ever ready for disaster to strike. No matter what my parents did wrong, they did one thing right. They gave me a lifejacket for life's stormy weather.

I was in church every time the doors were open, whether I liked it or not. Though some can go to church their entire lives and get nothing out of it, that wasn't the case for me. I memorized scripture verses and they became imbedded in my subconscious. To use religious jargon, I was baptized, catechized, and sanctified. I had a shield of faith and a sword of truth ready for whatever life could throw at me.

This is what I knew for sure: God would never leave me or forsake me, everything would work for good because I love God and am called for His purpose, and nothing could separate me from God's love. He chose me to do good things that He planned long ago. As Kay Arthur says, "Because God is love and because God rules over all, everything that comes into our lives is filtered through His sovereign fingers of love."

This is what I don't know: why terrible things happen, why there are famines and natural disasters, diseases or mysterious tumors. None of it makes any sense to me. I only know that death doesn't win, Love does. Sometimes life is painful and so is love, but it is always worth it. Even in the most hopeless of situations, there is always hope, because of Love.

Sometimes the loving thing hurts, like washing an open wound with saline solution. The burning pain can be excruciating, but it's only temporary and will prevent a nasty infection. I viewed my condition in a similar way. This was a painful situation, but hopefully a temporary one. An all knowing God was not caught by surprise by my diagnosis. He planned to use it for my good, I just didn't know how.

Ben thought I was able to sleep and not be anxious or stressed because I lost my memory and didn't know to be stressed out. He thought I was blissfully unaware of what might lay ahead but I wasn't. God's spirit gave me a profound peace. Something inside me told me that I could trust the author of my biography to write an inspirational story, something with a redemptive and uplifting theme, filled with triumph, not despair.

He didn't bring me through my life's history for it to end with a massive brain tumor. I felt confident that my story would have a different ending. God gave me assurance that His grace would be sufficient and I could let go of my need to know how, where, or why, for the time being.

I lost my need to pretend that I wasn't broken or that I didn't need help. After a lifetime of worrying about my outward appearance and what people thought of me, I let it go. I was a mess, everyone knew it, and I could finally accept the help available to me. It took Ben a little longer to get to there, but he did eventually. We both saw that where we were weak, God provided someone who was strong.

Being a Christ follower is not something you do alone. It is more than a personal relationship with God, it is a communal relationship with other followers. When we become believers, we are adopted into a family, grafted into a tree, and made a part of a body from which we can't be amputated. The ear can't say to the eye, "I don't need you." We all need each other. It's sometimes painful to be the weak and needy one, but it's only in our weakness that we can see God's strength and provision through other people. What an incredible provision it turned out to be.

CHAPTER 8

*"It's the same way, Corrie, with knowledge.
Some knowledge is too heavy for children. When
you are older and stronger, you can bear it. For
now you must trust me to carry it for you."*
— *Corrie ten Boom, The Hiding Place*

On Monday morning, we got up early and caught the ferry from Bremerton to Seattle. Opera Girl took us out for breakfast to a colorful café in the University district covered in bright paintings of musicians. We had some time to kill so she drove us through the nicer neighborhoods and stopped at an overlook so we could get a view of the city and take pictures. Ben and I posed next to an abstract sculpture overlooking the water. I thought it odd that we were talking vacation photos on our way to visit a neurosurgeon.

As we drove by fancy houses in an upscale area, OG told us who lived in a few of them and what they did for a living. Some she knew personally through her musical and political contacts. Some were local legends.

Then she told me about a couple people we both knew from college. I looked over at her as she cheerfully reported on their lives and said, "OG, I don't give a $#!* about any of those people or how their lives turned out. They so don't matter right now. Can we just go to the doctor's office already?" Ben chuckled from the back seat. My filters had completely broken down.

We arrived at the University of Washington Medical Center with time to spare so we wandered the building a bit. Light streamed from all directions and art pieces adorned the walls and waiting areas. The building sparkled, modern and clean. I felt like Dorothy visiting the Emerald City to see the Wizard of Oz. Entering such an opulent place leaves the impression that the people there must know what they are doing, which is probably why they spent so much on the building.

We found the neurosurgery clinic and waited for our appointment with the neurosurgeon. A nurse led us to an exam room after having me step on a scale and record my weight. She took my blood pressure and temperature and left us to wait for the doctor. OG pulled out her iPod and searched for some music to entertain us while we waited. Between classical opera and country twang, there wasn't anything she had that I wanted to hear.

We got to talking about our parents music and I thought of a Canadian singer with a rich, alto tone with texture like melted chocolate: smooth, rich, and creamy. We tried to think of all the artist's songs we had ever heard and started singing them. "Dancing in the moonlight, Darling, I'll meet you after midnight…." She sang a lot of really stupid love songs, but with her deep and soothing voice, she made them sound good.

A knock at the door interrupted our concert. A large, imposing man with broad shoulders and big torso entered the room, filling the space with his presence. He spoke with a deep, authoritative voice as he introduced himself and shook hands with each of us. He sat down, asked how we were doing, and then began to explain what my tumor was and how he was going to remove it.

He called the tumor a craniopharyngioma, a small solid benign mass surrounded by a cyst collecting fluid. He explained that they are usually found in children because they are present at birth and grow slowly over time. He described the cyst as a pinched off piece of matter that collected fluid. Even though the hard part of the tumor grew very slowly, the cyst was probably growing more quickly, which would explain the sudden onslaught of symptoms.

He said memory loss was not typically caused by this kind of tumor but could be caused by the cyst. The lining part of the cyst might be pressing on the optic nerve, hypothalamus, pituitary and carotid artery. He couldn't know for sure until he got in there and removed it.

As he was describing the tumor, I tried to break into his spiel to ask questions, but he wouldn't let me. "You can ask questions when I'm done explaining your condition," he said, sternly.

I was afraid I would forget what I was going to ask, but he was getting visibly irritated with me and my interruptions. Ben and OG would shush me as soon as I opened my mouth to speak. I was afraid my questions would fly out of my head as fast as they flew in. Ben did his best to digest what the doctor was telling him and OG took notes like a mad woman. I tried to calm myself with the thought that I could quiz her when the appointment was over.

He prescribed a maximally invasive surgery called an orbitozygomatic craniotomy. It required an incision across the scalp from ear to ear. The surgeon would remove the bone that forms the contour of the eye orbit and cheek and replace it at the end of surgery. Temporarily removing this bone would allow him to reach the deep insides of the brain where the tumor was located without causing severe damage to the surrounding brain tissue.

The doctor didn't know how all of the surrounding areas would be affected until he got in there and saw how easily the cyst and the mass could be removed. The lining of the cyst could either peel away easily or not so easily. Another consideration was that this type of tumor and cyst tends to act like a weed and come back over and over. This surgery would deal with the immediate and later we would focus on the long-term, which could include radiation treatment.

"Our doctor at home said something about a gamma knife laser that could be used in place of surgery. What about that?" Ben inquired. I was wondering the same thing.

"Because of the size and location of the cyst, radiation alone is not an option. This case requires surgery," the doctor replied.

"What's going to happen to my hair? Will you shave my head and leave a huge scar?" I didn't want to look like a bald monster if at all possible.

The doctor smiled and explained that they shave just a one inch strip at the incision site and leave the rest alone. "You'll leave surgery with most of your hair and a band of staples from ear to ear."

"What if I don't want to get surgery?" I asked, feeling defiant.

"If you don't want permanent memory loss, blindness, or possible death, you will have surgery."

"Well, when you put it that way. How long is this all going to take?"

"Surgery takes from 6 to 8 hours. If everything goes well, you will be in the hospital 3-5 days. If there are complications, you could be in the hospital for a week to ten days."

"What are the chances that I won't get better or that something worse will happen?"

"Ninety to ninety five percent of patients come out of surgery with positive outcomes and improved function."

"What about the gamma knife thingy? Could you use that?" I forgot that Ben already asked.

"Depending on how much of the tumor we leave behind, you may have gamma knife radiation AFTER surgery." The doctor assured us that he would get as much of the tumor out as possible, but that he might have to be a little conservative. The brain is delicate and he did not want to cause damage to the surrounding areas.

"Assuming everything goes well, how long until I'm back to my old self?"

"I can't answer that. We won't know until after surgery." That was the least satisfying answer of the day.

"How soon will she go in for surgery?" Ben asked, hoping I could get in by the end of the week.

"She isn't in immediate danger but the sooner we get this taken care of, the better. She will need a field vision test, a CT scan, and a pituitary function test before we operate. You can have those done at home. We'll schedule the surgery a few weeks from now."

Ben scribbled down the list of tests and scans I needed to have and got the information on where to send the results. He taped business cards from the doctor and the nurse care coordinator in his notebook. "My nurse will be your contact. Call her with any questions you may have."

We had just been told I needed major brain surgery in three weeks but no one mentioned what I would be doing in the meantime, besides taking tests. I had lots of questions.

"Can I still drive?"

"Probably not a good idea," he said.

"Can I post stuff on Facebook?" I asked.

I stumped him for a second. "You might want someone else to describe your condition to family and friends." It really didn't matter what he said. I was going to do whatever I wanted on Facebook anyway.

"Can I drink Mountain Dew when I get a headache? It seems to be the only thing that works."

"Absolutely. Mountain Dew works great for treating headaches."

"Seriously? You're telling me it's okay to drink Mountain Dew?"

"If that's what works for you, that's fine. Whatever you need to be comfortable."

I looked at Ben as if to say, "Did you hear that? A doctor prescribed Mountain Dew!"

OG, Ben and I all failed to ask how long it would take for me to recover from surgery, what damage surgery would do to my body, and what I could expect during my time in the hospital and beyond, or at least there was nothing in our notes about that discussion. It was as though knowing about the surgery was all we could carry at the time.

Corrie Ten Boom told a story about her father and how he chose to share information with his kids. He compared knowledge to luggage. He wouldn't tell his children anything too heavy for them to carry, just as he would not expect them to lift a 50 pound suitcase. Telling me what to expect during recovery would have probably been like giving me a steamer chest of heavy metal to drag home with me. The doctor gave me as much information as I could carry at the time and even then, I had to have it written down for me because most of what he said I did not remember.

I still didn't know what I was going to do with myself for the weeks prior to surgery. I would be sitting at home, drinking Mountain Dew, not driving or posting embarrassing stuff on Facebook. It all sounded so miserable. "What am I supposed to do between now and surgery?" I asked.

"Go home and have fun," the neurosurgeon said.

The doctor told Ben he would get a phone call with the scheduled date for surgery. We would have to return to Seattle a couple days prior to surgery for some final pre-op tests, but for now we were free to return home, get the needed tests done, and "have fun." He wrote "Have Fun" on a piece of paper, signed it "Dr. Bob" and handed it to me.

"That's funny," I said, not amused.

As much as I would like to say that I went home and "had fun", that didn't happen. I felt frustrated, useless, and confused. Now that I had a diagnosis, my pretending that I could fool people into thinking I was normal came to an end. I needed a sign I could wear that said, "I HAVE A BRAIN TUMOR" to excuse my strange behavior, my mood swings, and my lack of filters. I wanted a visual cue on my person so I didn't have to apologize for being offensive and annoying all the time. Being broken is no fun at all.

As much as I felt grateful for everything my husband and friends were doing to help me, I struggled with distrust, broken pride, and low self-esteem. It was hard watching the world keep turning without me. Instead of enjoying the break from the juggling of daily tasks, I swam in a mucky swamp of guilt and depression. I didn't know what I was supposed to be doing, who I was responsible for, or where I was supposed to be. The answers to those questions were nothing, no one, and nowhere in particular. Things were getting taken care of by people besides me and I didn't know how to feel about it.

I had been the family's chief financial officer, handling all the accounts and bill paying with Ben happily disconnected, trusting that I was taking care of everything. For weeks, I had difficulty reconciling the checkbook with our bank statement. Charges I didn't remember making appeared and mangled my accounting. At least now we knew why.

Our circumstances forced Ben to take a more active role in both our finances and our home life. I couldn't drive, so he changed his work schedule so that he could come home to pick up and drop off the girls at school. He also took charge of our money. In normal circumstances, I might have resisted giving up control, but given my condition, I gladly handed the checkbook over to my husband.

Ben wasn't sure what he would find when he looked into our spending. I had already ordered cable television and magazines without exactly remembering what I had done. To his pleasant surprise, I organized the finances in an idiot-proof way so my impulsive spending had done no damage. I set up two checking accounts, one for fixed expenses and one for variables. Automated payments from our fixed account covered our bills every month. We only had to track spending from the variable account which also held our emergency fund. Ben could easily keep track of what was going out of the account because I wasn't going anywhere spending money.

As Ben covered my responsibilities at home, other people covered my paid and volunteer obligations. The friend who previously had my job offered to take over my duties until I recovered from surgery. She came over and reviewed the meeting plans and bookkeeping software with me. I answered her questions as I repeated mine over and over. She graciously answered me each time as though it was the first. Meetings with the Friends of Library and the Crafty Cooks 4-H class were either cancelled or went on without me.

After we got home from Seattle, Ben made a habit of leaving notes on 3 X 5 cards that told me what the day of the month and week it was and something along the lines of, "Don't worry. You aren't responsible for anything. Relax and enjoy the day." These loving notes were not received in the spirit in which they were given. They made me even crazier than I already was. It was as though they read, "What you would usually do today isn't important or someone else can do it just as well. We don't need you so your worst fears have come true and you are officially worthless. Enjoy the day."

I confronted Ben and told him his little love notes were not working for me. "You need to stop with the index cards. I pretty much hate them."

"I thought they would be helpful. I figured they'd help you remember which day it is."

"We have a calendar. I can figure out what day it is. I have been for weeks now. Besides, it doesn't matter what day it is if I'm not doing anything. I don't know where anyone is or when they are coming home. I don't know what I'm supposed to be DOING."

"You don't need to know when the kids need picked up because I'm taking care of it."

"You aren't getting what I am saying. It doesn't matter that I'm not responsible for them. I still want to know. I want to matter. Give me a list of things to do."

"The doctor said you shouldn't be expected to do anything."

"Screw what the doctor said. GIVE ME A TO DO LIST!"

I preferred a list of household chores that I could check off rather than encouragement to rest and relax because I needed to feel productive. In an attempt to take away potential sources of stress, my family brought to the surface my greatest source of stress, being dispensable.

Like normal human beings, my husband and children got annoyed with me, sighed and rolled their eyes, and raised their voices when asked the same question sixteen times. I couldn't remember the content of what they told me, but I registered the tone they used when they spoke to me. If they expressed irritation with me, I felt hurt and angry. I was quick to lash out.

I constantly felt distrustful and mad. I wanted everyone to show me grace and patience, but I had none. I couldn't remember any of their thoughtful acts or words but every flippant or sarcastic comment was seared into my mind. I told my 13-year-old, "If I die, you are going to feel terrible about the way you've treated me." If a parent's role in a child's life is to give her something to talk about in therapy, I did my job. My emotions trumped the feelings of everyone else in our home. No one was "having fun."

I used my condition as a free pass to be a self-absorbed fool. Proverbs 14:1 says, "A wise woman builds her house; a foolish woman tears her house down with her own hands." I was tearing down my house with my bad attitude. I knew it was wrong, but felt powerless to do anything about it. I wanted to do what was right, but I inevitably did what was wrong.

It would seem like being prideful and having low self-esteem are on two ends of the emotional spectrum, but I struggled with both. I spent weeks spinning in circles, maintaining appearances, and refusing to admit my need because of pride. When the pretending came to an end, I was left with the realization that I wasn't as indispensable as I thought I was. I entangled my sense of self-worth with my ability to get things done. Both my pride and my low self-worth had become idols occupying space on my mental shelf. They filled my every waking thought. They needed to be taken off the altar of my mind and smashed.

I was the star of my own show; my family played a supporting role. I cast myself as the unappreciated, under-valued suffering servant to my selfish, entitled family. I did things for them because I loved them, but also because I wanted their praise and appreciation. When they got frustrated with me and stopped depending on me, it was like I got kicked off the stage; the show could go on without me. I wasn't the star after all. It was painful to lose everything I thought made me worthwhile and yet, I was still loved. Loved in spite of my unloveliness, I wallowed in self-pity, ignoring the grace that surrounded me.

CHAPTER 9

*Friends show their love in times of trouble, not
in happiness. - Euripides*

What snapped me out of my self-pity was seeing all the people walk into our chaos when I would have been inclined to walk away. Our whole community overwhelmed us with their love and support. As we walked on the wobbly tightrope of brain surgery, they provided a safety harness and net. Having their support alleviated many fears and worries.

Ben used all his paid leave from work during his illness and our initial trip to Seattle to see the neurosurgeon. He would have to take at least two more weeks off, if not more, during my hospitalization and recovery time. We weren't sure how we would pay for our medical bills, hotel and travel costs, or regular living expenses without him getting a paycheck during that time. The financial burden felt too heavy to bear.

People from Ben's work came up to him, ask him how the family was doing, and slipped money into his pocket as they left. His fellow employees and our church family collected money to help us with our travel and medical expenses. Friends even sent checks in the mail. I've never before experienced that much generosity from so many different people at one time.

It was like the final scene in the movie "It's A Wonderful Life" where all of George Bailey's friends come to his house and empty their pockets full of money to help George when he felt worthless and hopeless. George discovered he was the richest man in town and no one is a failure who has friends. Ben and I felt like George, overwhelmed by the wealth we didn't know we had.

A couple years ago, I competed in my first triathlon. The swimming portion covered a small section of a large lake and the wind made the water choppy and hard to navigate. The race began and I tumbled into the water with the rest of my group. It was like a scene from the Titanic: arms and legs flailing everywhere, heads bobbing in and out of the water. There was no swimming, just surviving. I did all I could to propel myself forward and keep from getting hit in the head or taking water into my lungs. I paddled my arms and kicked my legs, but it seems as though I was treading water and going nowhere.

Then, I saw a couple paramedics standing on a dock at the half-way point of the water course. I made it to the dock, grasped the edge, and stopped to catch my breath. After taking a couple deep breaths, one of EMTs leaned over and asked, "Are you doing okay?"

"I'm fine. I just needed to take a quick break," I said between gasps, gripping the dock for life.

"You're doing great. In about 100 feet, the water is shallow enough that you can walk the rest of the way to shore. You can do it."

That piece of information was all I needed to finish. I put everything I had into paddling to the shallow water and when I could feel sand under my toes, I ran to land and kept going until I got to my bike. The swim was the worst part of the triathlon and it lasted only ten minutes.

Our friends were like the paramedics standing on the dock, letting us know that they wouldn't let us drown. They brought our family meals, made sure I was not alone all day, and came to walk with me. They called to check on me, even if I forgot what they said immediately after I got off the phone with them. I had days where it seemed like my head was barely staying above water but after a little paddling and panic, there was always someone to remind me that I wouldn't be swimming in the deep forever.

A friend from Ben's work and his family offered to keep the girls for as long as necessary. They lived close to both girls' schools, had kids of similar ages, and had extensive hospital experience. Their oldest daughter was born with a heart defect. She is now a happy and healthy 11-year-old girl, but they knew what it is like to spend time in the hospital and see specialists far from home. They slipped Ben some cash and a case of Ensure, knowing he might not get an opportunity to eat a real meal during our hospital stay. It lifted a huge burden knowing that the girls would be taken care of.

As we travelled, Ben and I passed my cell phone back and forth. My friends still talked to me as though I could remember but ultimately, I had to hand the phone over to Ben so the content of the conversations wouldn't be lost. He handled the logistics of scheduling so I could meet with my West side friends before the big day.

We arrived at our hotel in Seattle on the evening of Sunday, April 21st both exhausted and relieved. As much as I dreaded the surgery and hospital stay, I looked forward to an end to the waiting. I was ready to get my memory back and return to life as it was before the depression and memory lost started. I felt hopeful as we looked forward to pre-op appointments on Monday, resting and visiting with friends and family on Tuesday, and surgery on Wednesday morning at 5:30am.

We stayed at the Collegianna, an old college dormitory converted to a hotel for patients of the University hospital system. Our room smelled musty and looked like a dingy 1980s dorm room with industrial flooring, large wood laminate furniture, and no mirrors. A desk with a hutch and a wide wardrobe divided the room in two, keeping the light from the windows on one side of the room from reaching the other. Three single beds, two more desks and wardrobes, and a television filled the space, leaving narrow aisles for walking. I picked the bed on the dark side, closest to the bathroom door while Ben slept on the other side of the divide, close to the windows. The mattress felt firm, but adequate. We got what we paid for, which wasn't much by Seattle standards.

The next morning, Opera Girl came and took us out for breakfast. I'd love to tell you where we went and what we said, but I don't recall. I just remember that my friend gave me a big hug, promised that she would return to visit after surgery, and said she would report back to my friends at home on my progress. I appreciated that she understood my desire to keep people updated on my status. Ben wasn't up for it.

Dealing with me and my social calendar in the midst of the greatest stress of his life proved difficult for my husband. When Ben is stressed, he doesn't want to talk through his problems or share his feelings. He doesn't need to vent or call his five closest friends to share his frustrations. In his mind, emotional connection correlates with physical proximity. However, feeling connected doesn't require engaging in conversation. Like my cat, he wants you in the room with him but not demanding interaction. When he's under pressure, like he was during my illness, he would prefer to converse with as few people as possible and keep things private.

Because Ben didn't share my need for social connection, it sometimes caused conflict between us. He refused to use Facebook and for a long time, resented the time I spent using the computer. He strongly believed that the people who used the internet to communicate with me did not matter. If they did, they would call or show up. I didn't think he was being fair at all.

After years of moving all over the country, I collected a few friends in each of the places we lived. My friends from high school and college had scattered throughout the country and there was no way I could keep in touch with everyone through visits and phone calls. It was unrealistic to expect that I could. By using the internet, I could get a glimpse into my friends' lives and share part of mine with them. Facebook became my link to the outside world and my means of maintaining lifelong friendships.

I also got to know more of my extended family through social media. I exchanged updates and messages with cousins I'd seen only a few times in my life. I became better acquainted with a cousin that lived in Seattle through Facebook. That day while we were eating breakfast, she sent a text asking if we would like to share a meal with her and her husband. That evening after my pre-op appointments, they took us to dinner at a steak house near the hospital. Their concern and generosity meant a lot to us and I counted them as a blessing that came from using the computer to connect. Ben didn't see it that way because they called and showed up. Therefore the computer had nothing to do with it. Showing up is what counted in his book.

Tuesday, the day before surgery, Ben's support team started to form. Ben's mom and dad decided to get a room at our hotel and stay until the surgery was over. Another friend, John, flew to Seattle to stay with Ben while he waited during surgery. John had surgery on his knee months earlier and was still recovering from it. Knowing the value of having someone physically present, he wanted to be there for Ben.

That same day, my friend Kathy drove from Olympia bearing gifts of fuzzy, warm socks, and hand lotion. She and I went shopping at a nearby strip mall and met Ben and his crew for lunch at Chipotle. After lunch, we walked with my mother-in-law to a frozen yogurt shop near the hotel and visited until Kathy had to drive home. I lived in a cloud of confusion, not sure when my surgery would happen, but our family and friends surrounded me with love, patience, and gentleness. I went to bed that night feeling cared for, prayed for, and loved.

CHAPTER 10

"I'm not happy to get surgery, but I'm happy
that I can focus on getting better."
– Dwyane Wade

We left for the hospital before the sun came up. We checked in at the reception area and almost immediately were led into a small room with a bed and a couple chairs. The nurse handed me a hospital gown and a large plastic bag, instructing me to put on the gown and put all my clothes into the bag. I followed her orders and hopped onto the bed. She came into the room and covered me with a blanket that inflated with warm air. Then, she quickly and efficiently inserted a couple IV lines into the back of my hand. She was so good I barely felt it. Someone else came and drew marks on my head and positioned monitors on my chest.

After they left, a slender, friendly looking Asian man in a white coat and name badge came into the room, smiling as he introduced himself. "My name is Winston and I am the resident anesthesiologist. I'm going to be taking care of you until you're ready for surgery."

"Winston? That's an unusual name. Are you named after someone?"

"Winston Churchill."

"Your mom named you after a British Prime minister?"

"Yeah. It's the kind of name most people give their bulldogs."

"Or children that they hope will become Anesthesiologists."

"Maybe so," he chuckled.

Winston moved me and my bed through the door of my room and stopped to talk to Ben. "The waiting area is through those double doors. The nurse you met earlier will give you a progress report in a few hours and the surgeon will speak with you when they're all done." Winston must have slipped me something before we left the pre-op room because I was already on my way to sleepy land when Ben kissed me goodbye. "Don't worry; we'll take good care of her," Winston reassured Ben as he pushed me down the hall. My bed glided through a labyrinth of turns and stopped inside an elevator. I remember thinking there was no way I could re-trace the route and then I fell asleep. I woke up in the Surgical Intensive Care Unit twelve hours later.

I opened my eyes to a wall of windows with the blinds closed but lights shining through them. The light made everything look gray like a black and white movie, except the red lights on the monitors next to my bed. Every few minutes a blood-pressure cuff around my arm or cuffs around my calves would fill with air and squeeze me. "Beep, Beep, Beep," the machines sounded as they released pressure. I could hear beeping coming from my open door too. Beeping sounds surrounded me.

Relief and gratitude washed over me in those first few conscious moments. I felt groggy, but not confused or disoriented. I knew where I was and what had happened. Though numbed by medicine, I knew I was alive and able to think clearly again. I gingerly slid my hand, covered in tape and tubes, along the side of my head. My hair stuck to the side of my face, covered in goo. I felt where my hair ended but didn't dare touch any further in fear of contaminating my wound. I didn't feel any pain on the top of my head at all, but my face felt like someone had punched me with iron knuckles.

When I opened both of my eyes, I saw two of everything: Two clocks on the wall, two television screens, and two doorways into the room. If I closed my right eye, my vision cleared and returned to normal. It felt weird to only use my left eye, but the double vision made my eyes tired and sore.

Shortly after I gained consciousness, two men in their 20s came into the room. "My name is Thad," said the tall one with short brown hair and a pock marked face. He turned to his colleague, a smaller man with Asian eyes and a broad nose. "This is Marvell."

"That's an uncommon name. Are you named after someone?" I asked.

"A British poet," he said.

"I've never heard of him."

"Uh, he was pretty famous. You can Google him later."

"Hey, I just met a guy before surgery named Winston. You're both named after British guys." And they were both Asian, but I didn't mention that. They really didn't look that much alike.

"What is your pain level right now?" Thad asked.

"It's probably a five, but mostly right behind my eye."

"I can give you an Oxycodone now and another in three hours. I can give you a couple Tylenol too. Would you like both?"

"Sure, why not?"

They let Ben know that I was awake and he came to the room with his parents. His mom leaned into to kiss my cheek and said they were heading home, happy to know the surgery went successfully. Ben wanted to get his bag and settle in the room with me but I insisted he go back to our hotel and get some sleep. I convinced him that he would be a much better support to me if he was rested. He reluctantly agreed and said he would return first thing in the morning.

I tried to go back to sleep but it was nearly impossible. It was like Christmas morning when it's too early for opening presents. My eyes longed for rest but my head buzzed with random activity and anticipation. My mind could not turn off as it fell into fitful bouts of sleep filled with strange dreams. My circadian rhythms were all wacky and I wanted to start a new day at midnight.

To make sure there are no changes in brain function during the hours following surgery, every hour a nurse would wake me and ask "What day is it?", "Where are you?", and "Why are you here?" Then, he would ask me to squeeze his fingers, push his hands away, puff my cheeks, and wiggle my toes. Each time I took the test I passed, even though I cheated by squinting to read the white board hanging on the wall in front of me. It had the day written in bold letters at the top. I had been out of surgery for only a few hours, but it felt like a week. Every hour seemed like a day.

The unit buzzed with activity. Doors to patient rooms were left open with just a curtain pulled for privacy. Conversations in the hallway, pop songs playing on the radio at the nurses' station, and heavy footsteps exiting the elevator echoed through the room. When I closed my eyes to rest, the sounds surrounding me entered my dreams, making me feel like I was hallucinating. I kept thinking that someone was going to walk into the room at any moment and I would need to be alert.

Well after midnight, an aid from radiology woke me for a post-surgery MRI. He helped me into a wheelchair and transported me to the second floor. Barely awake and thinking it was morning, I chatted with the aid as we traveled through the halls. After the technician completed the scan, the aid wheeled me back to my room. Nurse Thad came and helped me return to bed and told me to go back to sleep.

"I am so glad I have my brain back. My husband is going to be relieved that I'm back to normal again," I told the nurse.

"Really? Are you sure about that?" he responded, seemingly unconvinced that I was normal.

"Yes, and I'm not sleepy," I responded, feeling a little obstinate. "I've technically been asleep all day, given that I was wheeled into surgery in the morning and didn't wake until night time."

"Your blood pressure is too high. You need to relax and get some rest," the nurse lectured. "You need to stop talking because every time you talk, your blood pressure goes up."

He kept talking to me and reprimanding me when I responded. He was like that annoying dentist that asks questions while they have their hands in your mouth and then gets upset when you try to answer them. "Be quiet and go to your happy place in your mind," he said.

"I would, but my happy place isn't being tied to a hospital bed, hearing whispers of bad pop music. Could you tell the nurses across the hall to turn the radio down?"

"Don't worry about that. Listen, I'm going to teach you a natural way to lower your blood pressure. Take deep, slow breaths. Think about relaxing your entire body," he instructed.

"I am relaxed." I closed my eyes but it did no good. "I think my happy place raises my blood pressure." All my happy places: white water rafting, flying down water slides, singing on stage, are not exactly activities that cause a decrease in blood pressure. I tried to imagine a boring place instead.

As I thought about being anywhere other than where I was, I started to cough and couldn't stop. All the moisture in my mouth evaporated. I felt like one of those Looney tunes cartoons where the character is traveling through the desert in search of an oasis and ends up eating sand. "I'm thirsty....really thirsty. I need water, please!"

"We can't give you any water. You have tests being taken that are food and drink sensitive," said the evil nurse from hell.

"Seriously, I'm dying!" I've never experienced such extreme desire for water or any liquid for that matter.

"I'll check to see if you can have ice chips."

It seemed like hours before Marvell returned with a cup of ice and a spoon. He took a spoon full of ice and put it in my mouth. It was the most glorious feeling I've ever had. The smooth, flat chips melted into pools of refreshing water that trickled down my parched throat. Never had such a desperate need been satisfied by something so small and seemingly insignificant. I felt an overwhelming sense of gratitude for this gesture of kindness.

"I feel SO MUCH BETTER. I will never take ice chips for granted ever again. Thank you, Winston."

"My name isn't Winston. It's Marvell." Oops. I would accidently call him Winston several times during the night.

Something in my brain would only let me hold one uncommon name at a time. The other staff thought my calling him Winston was hilarious; Marvell was less amused. I had no trouble remember the name of the chatty nurse that annoyed me but for Marvell's name, my mind went blank. I tried to make a mental note, obscure British poet, not famous British prime minister.

The night continued to go downhill from there. After getting some minor relief from the ice chips, I threw up all over myself. I pressed the call button on my bedside remote and Nurse Thad came a few moments later. "Was it projectile vomit?" he asked, as though there was another kind.

"It came without warning, if that's what you mean," I replied, confused by the question. What other kind of vomit is there? I had to be washed from the neck down. The entire bed striped and gown replaced. He gave me an anti-nausea medication, but the damage was done.

At that point, I was glad Ben was asleep in his bed far away. In his attempts to be helpful, he can go overboard with hovering and questioning concern. He could also get easily flustered. Once, he wanted to drive me to the hospital when I had a bout of morning sickness combined with a box of Red Vines. I took me awhile to convince him that I wasn't vomiting blood.

He also nearly fainted when I labored with both our children. We wore matching oxygen masks. He thought I'd lost a major organ when I delivered the placenta after our first daughter was born. He asked the doctor if that was something that needed to be put back. I remembered how upset he got and thought that sending him home was the right decision. At least he wasn't here, stressing everyone with his tendency to over-react.

Then, something else gross happened. I passed gas and felt something not a part of me touch my skin. I panicked a little, afraid to move. One of the nurses came into the room to perform the hourly check.

"I think I might have pooped," I nervously told him.

"That's never happened before," he said, barely hiding his disgust at the thought. I couldn't believe that I was the first person in the history of the SICU to accidently poop. The nurse rolled my body to check under my bottom.

"You're good," he said, with more than a little relief in his voice.

"That's weird," I said. I still felt something that shouldn't be there, a phantom poop. It bothered me and I couldn't stop thinking about how uncomfortable I was and how Ben was somewhere in a soft bed, sleeping peacefully.

My mind switched from kind, warm thoughts toward him to angry, resentful thoughts. My mind flooded my body with emotions that held little grasp on reality. My brain let me know it was agitated by the surgery and it was taking it out on my husband. The poor guy didn't know what he was in for when he stepped into the hospital room the next morning, a few hours later than I expected.

Morning came and it was time for doctor's rounds, when the neurosurgery team visits all their patients on the floor to answer questions and discuss the course of treatment during recovery at the hospital. I woke up too early, feeling bored and agitated. I couldn't watch television or read because of the double vision and the pain behind my eyes, especially on the right side. I felt like I had been in a boxing match all night and I asked for an ice pack to put on my face. The cold numbed the pain better than any of the medications I was taking but I couldn't go back to sleep.

Alone inside my head was a dangerous place to be. Nervous and upset because Ben had not arrived, I fretted all morning. I expected him to be there shortly after I woke. I worried the doctors would come, give important information, and I wouldn't be able to remember. My memory had returned but my confidence was still missing. I wanted someone else to still be responsible for me. Even though my mind felt back to normal, I still wanted someone else to be paying attention to what was being said.

I couldn't call Ben on the hospital room's phone because our long-distance phone number required a special code. I asked a nurse to call our cell phone and tell Ben to come and bring Mountain Dew with him. He called and there was no answer, so he left a message. I tried not to worry. It wasn't yet eight o'clock.

When eight thirty rolled around, the doctors arrived but Ben had not. I seethed, imagining him having a leisurely breakfast with his friend John instead of being with me where he belonged. The sleep deprivation gave me the attention span of a gnat and I longed for a can of Mountain Dew to make me feel normal. I felt like an addict, waiting for her next fix.

The rounds with the neurosurgery team helped me understand the condition I was in. They asked how I was feeling, looked at my incision, and discussed my sodium levels. I drank water constantly and could feel it go into my mouth and through my digestive track in an instant. It didn't stop to say hi to any other part of my body, it just ran right through.

"I was dying of thirst last night and they wouldn't give me anything to drink," I lamented to the surgical team.

"I'm sorry about that. They could have given you water. I think there may have been a misunderstanding about that. We restrict food and drinks after surgery, but it isn't necessary to withhold water," one of the doctors told me. I felt irritated and resentful.

The doctor continued and explained that I had diabetes insipidus, which means the body has difficulty regulating fluid levels. He said the steroid I was given to prevent swelling caused high blood pressure and high blood sugar. My blood sugar would be checked before each meal and I would be given insulin as needed. Nothing would be done about my blood pressure unless it went above 160 over something. Thad made me feel like the high blood pressure was my fault because I didn't sleep and talked all night. I was relieved to find out that it wasn't anything I was doing.

When Ben finally arrived after 9 am, I was livid. "Did you get your phone messages?"

"What messages? The phone is in John's bag."

"How is anyone supposed to get a hold of you if you don't have the phone?"

"I don't want anyone getting a hold of me. I'm sick of answering the phone. That's why it's in John's bag!"

"What about me? I'm lying in a hospital bed while you are out doing who knows what. How am I supposed to get a hold of you?"

"I didn't think you'd be up very early. The nurse last night said the doctors do their rounds from 9am – 1pm. I didn't want to disturb you."

"Well, you missed rounds by 30 minutes. I feel like you think this is a vacation or something. You have your parents and John to hang out with while I'm getting my head cut open. There's no one here for me."

"They are here for you, too. None of us would be here if it weren't for you."

"Well I want someone here on my team. Call my brother. He'll come."

"What are you talking about? There are no teams. Everyone loves you as much as they love me."

I gave him the look that said, "Who are you kidding?"

He relented. "I will get the phone and call Scott."

CHAPTER 11

*Everyone feels benevolent if nothing happens to
be annoying him at the moment.*
– C.S. Lewis, <u>The Problem of Pain</u>

Ben left to get the cell phone out of his friend's bag, check
out of the hotel, and get me a case of Mountain Dew. I continued to
fume in his absence. My only relief came from ice packs and
medication. The pain killers flowing through my veins made my
head float above my body like a helium balloon. The wall in front of
me seemed like the ceiling and I couldn't tell up from down. My
body didn't feel like my own. I didn't recognize the pale white
doughy form, soft and shapeless. I felt like a hideous mess. My hair
was tangled and caked with blood and goo. I smelled metallic and
sweaty. Tape, tubes, and bags of fluid chained me to the bed. My
whole body felt like an itch that could not be scratched. The
irritation occupied my every thought.

A nameless resident came to remove the drain line from my
head. He described it as a long spaghetti noodle sliding along the
side of my head, just under the skin. The quick removal went

smoothly but left behind a string of slime down my hairline. He left without so much as wiping my face, adding another layer of goop in my already greasy hair. Feeling a little high from the painkillers, I didn't react to the indignity until the slime dried and cemented blood and hair to my ear and cheek.

This thoughtless, minor neglect of wiping away the ooze added insult to injury. The 64 staples in my head could not be avoided. The swollen, black eye was inevitable. The tubes, the needles, and the cuffs were all required. But, letting my hair stick to my face in a mat of goo and blood seemed cruel. I lost my humanity and became a task on some over-worked medical student's to do list. It hurt to be treated like an object that needed a drain line removed, unworthy of attention and care.

Ben returned with a case of Mountain Dew, explaining that he had to drive three miles away to a convenience store. I grabbed the can from his hand and immediately gulped it down. Instead of saying thank you, I continued the rant I hadn't finished earlier that morning.

"Did you text BFF with status updates so she could post on Facebook?"

"Screw Facebook. I'm done with talking to people."

"You said you would text BFF so she could post my progress on Facebook."

"I never said that."

"If you don't want people calling or texting all day, we need to have someone giving status updates. Give me the phone. Ben, there are eight unanswered texted messages and four voice mails. Two of those voice mails are me. When was the last time you checked the phone?"

"I don't know, sometime before I went to bed. You know, you could just turn the phone off again. No one will die if they don't know what's happening."

"Whatever."

I closed one eye and went through the texts from my friends. After confirming that I was alive and well, two of them asked me about my hair. It's no wonder I obsessed about my appearance. The first question I get out of surgery is, "How's your hair?" I probably shouldn't have been texting with double vision and dopey on pain killers, but having a brain tumor never stopped me. Ben certainly wasn't going to do it for me. He acted annoyed I was on the phone and ignoring him. I was still angry at him for having a good night's sleep and not answering the phone when I called.

"I was up coughing all night. I don't want to ever hear about how your coughing is allergies to my cat unless you actually get tested for allergies. Those morons at your work that cough all over the place and say it's allergies are idiots. They all have colds, they spread them to you, and you gave one to me," I ranted as I squinted at my phone.

I looked up and saw Ben's face. His expression read like I had just stabbed him in the heart. He didn't respond or defend himself. He looked at me with hurt in his eyes. At that point I realized I couldn't keep treating him this way, with disdain and disrespect. Even though he turned off the phone and showed up late, he was doing everything in his power to be kind and helpful. I repaid him by being mean and demanding. Something inside me clicked and remorse washed over me.

"I'm sorry. It's not your fault I had a bad night. I'll try to be nicer." I realized after a day or two passed that Ben didn't give me a cold because the coughing lasted only one night, as fluid drained down my throat from surgery. And he was right about the phone. No one had died from him declining to answer text messages. The world of my adoring fans could wait to hear about my misery.

After lunch, my brother came to visit. We joked about the ill effects of pain medication as a physical therapist came to talk to me about how to move during recovery. She had me sit up in my bed and stand with assistance. She gave me an additional gown to cover by backside. As he helped me put it on, Ben looked down and discovered a gigantic bandage the size of a greeting card stuck to the top of my bottom. He peeled it off and I immediately felt wiped clean. The phantom poop feeling was gone. I imagine the bandage was there to prevent a hot spot or sore from developing, but it seemed stupid to have a sticker closing the top of my butt. I don't know why the nurse didn't removed it or at least explain what had caused the strange sensation the night before.

Trying to stand, my lack of balance and coordination shocked me. The physical therapist wrapped a belt around my mid-section and had my husband and brother stand on either side to provide support. One held on to the belt behind me as I took my first steps to the hallway. I walked like a wobbly toddler, awkwardly shifting my weight from one foot to another. After one lap to the end of the hall and back, I needed a break. I felt dizzier than ever. I needed to get off the oxycodone if I was going to be able to walk out of the hospital.

All night long, vampires from the phlebotomy lab came to suck my blood. The lines already inserted in my hand worked for putting fluids and medication in, but didn't allow the technicians to take blood out. A nurse tried to "flush" one of the lines but all that did was make my veins hurt. It seemed easier to have my blood drawn with a needle. With my arm all pale and puffy, it was hard to find a vein. I appreciated the skilled technicians that could insert the needle quickly, draw the blood, and pull it out with only a tiny hole left behind. The less experienced ones made the whole experience painful and left bruises in their wake. One phlebotomist came in the night and couldn't find a vein. She poked me three times before she gave up and called someone else. I stayed awake for an hour getting my blood drawn. I felt like an exhausted human pin cushion.

Friday morning during rounds, the surgical team commented on how "good" I looked. "Your incision is healing nicely and your eye looks really good. Usually after this surgery, it would swell shut, but yours is still able to open."

"I have ice on it most of the day," I responded, proud of myself for asking for it.

"Wow. That ice made a huge difference. We should make using ice packs standard procedure from now on."

I couldn't believe ice wasn't already part of their treatment plan. Every high school sports trainer knows that ice is the first thing you use to treat an injury. There was something else I thought should be standard. "My hair is disgusting. Couldn't you guys have cleaned me up a little bit instead of leaving all this blood and goo behind?"

The head resident acted amused. "I'm sorry about that. I guess we were more concerned about saving your life than protecting your hair. We'll see about having someone clean it for you."

As rounds continued, the endocrinologists said they were not going to treat my diabetes insipidus because it could clear on its own. It's not uncommon for the pituitary gland to temporary stop working and then start again. They wanted to wait and see what would happen. The head resident told me that since my vision had improved and I was able to stand and walk, I would probably move out of ICU soon. They just needed to remove my catheter and find a bed on the crowded surgical floor.

I immediately started bugging the nursing staff about removing the catheter so I could get out of there. The doctor in charge of the surgical ICU, not one of my doctors, cautioned that I may want to keep it awhile longer because of how much fluid I was passing. "Because of your diabetes insipidus, you are going to be up and down all day long and it may have to go back in," he explained. "Let's wait a bit longer and see how things go."

I quit bugging the nurses but still felt anxious to get out of the hospital as soon as possible. I couldn't sleep, the food tasted terrible, and the nurse on duty that day was awful. He handed me a pill in a cup and said, "Here. Take this."

"What am I taking?"

"It's Prilosec, for heartburn."

"I don't have any heartburn."

"It's on the list of medications the doctor ordered. You must need it. Just take the pill."

"Can I speak with the doctor?"

"The doctor is busy."

"Okay, then I will wait until he isn't busy and he can explain why I've been prescribed a medicine for something I don't have."

The nurse made a huff sound and walked out of the room. He didn't bother with the hourly checks anymore. An occupational therapist paid a visit and showed me how to put on my pants and brush my teeth without bending over. I would not be allowed to lean over for the next six weeks while my skull healed. I quit taking the oxycodone and drank Mountain Dew with my Tylenol to keep the headache at bay. I hurt a little more but my head didn't feel disconnected from my body anymore. I could shuffle across the floor (with someone holding my arm) and not feel like I might lose my balance and fall.

My brother came to visit again and asked if his wife could come visit the next day when she was off work.

"Of course she can. Why would I say no?"

"Well, some people are sensitive about people seeing them in the hospital. She just wanted to make sure it was alright with you."

"Yes. It's alright with me. I'd love to see her," I assured him, wondering how badly I would have to look to not want to see my sister-in-law. I wasn't exactly comfortable with my situation but I wanted to see people. I complained about my hair situation to anyone who would listen. A janitor came into the room and I mistook her for the promised staff person who would clean my face and hair. She didn't speak English well but mumbled something about God's goodness as she left with the trash. I felt so stupid.

Then, a sweet young nursing student came to my room. She heard my plight and came armed with a comb, brush, and hair band. She gently worked the tangles out of my hair, removing the dried blood and disinfectant. Once she was able to run a comb through, she French braided the back, avoiding the line of staples along the top. With the hair pulled back, the interwoven strips of metal looked like an intricate headband. She was like an angel, sent from God.

Later that afternoon, another nurse came and said I could get my catheter out. Once it was removed, with Ben's help, I started getting out of bed to use the restroom. Unfortunately, it wasn't private. It was shared with the room next door. The thin, hollow wood door provided no sound barrier. We could hear the people talking in the room next door as though they were in the bathroom with us. I heard something about a misshaped skull and a need for a helmet. The description started to turn graphic.

"Shuffle your feet or make some white noise. I don't want to hear their conversation." Ben quickly obliged. This was love in action: He walked me to the bathroom, got the toilet paper ready for me, and made quiet noise to cover sounds from the neighboring room. That moment proved I made the right choice when I married him. When we were dating, I told him that I worried I could get cancer like my mom did. I warned him I might one day get fat, sick, and cranky and asked would he still love me. He said he hoped that would never happen but yes, he would. He kept his promise.

That night, we transferred to a regular hospital room. Thad and Marvell were on duty again. I wasn't nearly as anxious or needy as I was that first night, but I still had hard feelings about Thad's brusque treatment and denying me water. I told Ben that he tortured me all night and blamed my talking for my high blood pressure. Thad told Ben that he thought I might have sustained some brain damage after surgery because of my lack of filters.

"No, that's just Sarah," Ben replied, with a smile.

"See I told you so!" I gloated. "I am back to normal."

Before we left, I apologized to Marvell for calling him Winston and thanked him for feeding me ice chips when I was dying of thirst. I didn't see Thad to tell him goodbye but he was probably relieved to see me go. The feeling was mutual.

CHAPTER 12

A Hospital is no place to be sick. - Samuel Goldwyn

Once I moved to the surgical recovery floor, I lost most of the beeping monitors, cuffs, and IV lines. The nurse on duty helped us get settled for the night, making a bed for Ben from a fold-out chair next to the window. She brightened when we told her we were from Eastern Washington. "I am too!" she said excitedly. "I'm from Cle Elem. People from the Eastside are so much nicer, don't you think?"

I didn't want to break the news to her that Cle Elem isn't technically on the East side of the state because she seemed convinced that it was. She talked about the joys of small town life and the homesickness she felt for friendlier people. "People in the city push their dogs around in baby carriers and act like human children are a plague," she said. "I just don't understand it." Once we were done swapping Seattle horror stories, she made sure we had enough bedding and ice water then left us to rest saying, "Call me if you need anything."

My room faced the nurses' station. While I could hear the

sound of quiet conversation, it was a vast improvement over the incessant beeping in the SICU. Sometime in the night, I had a bad dream and called for Ben. A wave of relief washed over me when he answered. I couldn't see him but I knew he was there and I could go back to sleep.

The next morning, I assessed the new room. It was smaller, but had a private restroom. Without the tubes and cuffs tying me down, I could get up and use it without help. The white board posted on the wall in front of my bed listed the things I needed to do in order to be able to go home. I had to feed myself, dress myself, walk five times a day, and go number two. I felt confident I could already do the first two tasks. I made it my mission to accomplish the second two.

As I sat on the edge of my bed, waiting a moment before I stood to use the bathroom, I caught a glimpse of myself in the mirror. My other room didn't have a mirror, which was a good thing. My face looked misshaped and grotesque; one eye was bigger than the other. The braided hair could not make up for the bruises and line of shaved skin and staples across my head. I sobbed. Ben tried to comfort me. "It's only temporary."

The day shift nurse came in to see why I was crying. His response made me smile. "Honey, you look like a beauty queen compared to some of my other patients. They look REALLY bad and it isn't going to get much better for them. It will for you. Just give it time."

Not satisfied with the encouragement from the nurse, I called BFF to tell her the horrors of recovery and how no one warned me that I wouldn't be able to see straight, walk straight, or look in the mirror without crying.

"The doctor probably did warn you and you just don't remember."

"Quit being mean. I won't be able to do anything for weeks. The occupational therapist said I'm not allowed to bend. I can't load or unload the dishes or the laundry. I can't pick anything up. I can barely dress myself."

"You're going to be fine. You have your family. They can do all those things. It will be good for them to not be dependent on you. They need to learn to take responsibility."

"I think there are better ways to teach responsibility than having brain surgery. I'm miserable."

"It's not that bad," she said, trying to be encouraging but coming across as insensitive and callous.

"I gotta go. Nurse is here," I lied. I couldn't spend another minute on the phone with her. She made me so mad with her lack of sympathy and "this will be good for your family" talk I wanted to poke her eyes out with a shrimp fork.

Opera Girl called and asked if there was anything I wanted from the store before she came to visit. I asked her to bring some dry shampoo since I wasn't allowed to get my head wet. She came an hour later with the promised shampoo, candy, and People magazine, a staple at her house. It still hurt to read, but I could amuse myself by thumbing through the pages. She took pictures of me looking constipated but promised not to post them on the internet. She insisted I might want to document my journey someday. "I will never want to remember trying to poop in order to leave the hospital."

"I'll email them to you anyway. You never know."

"You're right. I need a before picture to put next to the after. Any photograph of me after this point is bound to be an improvement."

OG left and my brother Scott and his wife Monica stopped by. I complained to them until two of my doctors arrived for daily rounds. The entourage wasn't with them because it was a Saturday. They introduced themselves to my visitors and asked how I was feeling. "Ready to go home," I told them.

They said it was possible I could be discharged in a day or two but, I would need someone with me 24 hours for the first two weeks. Ben and I brainstormed aloud who we could ask to babysit me while he was at work. Scott volunteered to come home with us and stay with me during the day. I was surprised but grateful; I couldn't believe he would do that for me. It would be the most time we had spent together since he graduated from high school when I was eight.

By the end of the day, I completed all the tasks written on the white board. My nurse commented the next morning that he was sad to see me go. "You're my favorite patient; you're the only one who can dress, eat, and toilet by yourself."

"Thank you. I hope your other patients get better soon."

"I do too!' he said with a smile as he left.

With my discharge papers signed and my prescriptions filled, we left the hospital on Sunday afternoon and picked my brother up at his apartment. He brought me a pair of dark glasses to wear. My eyes weren't used to the brightness of the sky. After an hour on the road, we stopped to get something to eat. I wanted to be invisible, for no one to see me wobbly and helpless, wearing dark glasses and sporting staples across my head. When we got back to the car, I told Ben and Scott I wasn't ready to see people. I needed to get some sleep. I hoped the self-consciousness would pass in time. I wanted to stop caring so much about how I looked, but it wasn't easy when I saw glimpses of my puffy, bruised face in the car's side view mirror.

It was a little after 8 pm when we arrived in Walla Walla. I felt beaten and exhausted, even though I slept most of the five hour drive home. I just wanted to crawl into a warm, dark hole and not come out until I looked and felt well again. I knew the girls would be excited to have us home again. They missed being in their own house, in their own rooms, sleeping in their own beds. They missed their mom and dad too. I missed them but I wasn't ready for them. I felt too weak and broken to be anyone's mother right then.

We dropped my brother off at his hotel and called the couple that were caring for our girls and let them know that we were home. I asked if the girls could stay one more night but I was overruled by everyone else. When they came in the house, I sat on the couch propped up on pillows, half conscious and half sleeping. I heard them rush through the front door yelling, "MOM!"

They entered the family room and fell silent. They looked as though they had seen a monster, their eyes full of terror and fear. They weren't prepared for what brain surgery would look like. No one told them my face would be purple and yellow with bruises, I would have staples across my head, and one eye would look bigger than the other. They started weeping and ran to me, burying their faces in my chest. Their bodies shook as they sobbed loudly but didn't say anything. I took a deep breath and sighed. "Come on, guys. Stop," I said as I held them. "I know I'm hideous, but it's not as bad as it looks."

"They aren't crying because of how you look. They're crying because they missed you and are happy to see you," my husband said, a little annoyed with my lack of sensitivity.

"These are not happy tears," I said feeling self-conscious and unable to comfort them. "Guys, come on now. Stop it," I told them, all the while holding back my own tears.

"Let your mom rest. She's tired. It's time for bed," their dad instructed.

They reluctantly sulked away, sniffling and wiping their faces. "You'll see me in the morning. I love you," I called to them as they left the room.

My brother arrived first thing in the morning as Ben left for work. He helped the girls get their lunches together and they rode their bikes to school. I observed the morning commotion from my perch on the couch. I watched cable television and dozed off throughout the day. My brother sat with me, brought me drinks and food, and made sure I didn't try to get up too quickly.

He provided a hedge for me from curious eyes, stopping by with flowers and food. Gradually my defensiveness crumbled as I longed to see the faces that belonged to the voices in the entryway. "It's okay! I'm awake! You can come in!" I'd holler as my brother tried to tell them I wasn't up for visitors. It was just a matter of time before loneliness and boredom conquered vanity and pride. Though I feared my appearance might startle, I think everyone imagined the worst for me. Over and over I heard, "You look great considering you just had surgery." It took me awhile to believe it but eventually I did. I learned to extend myself the grace others gave me.

The staff at the city library and my church group coordinated meals every night for the first two weeks of my recovery. It seemed like everyone in town brought us something to eat. Love filled our kitchen counter in the form of potato casserole, macaroni and cheese, roast beef sandwiches, and chicken a la king. Name a fattening comfort food and I ate it, with abandon. For someone who barely left the couch, I felt famished a few hours after eating. I had the appetite of a teenage boy. I still had an unquenchable thirst and my brother graciously kept me supplied with fluids. I didn't want to drink Mountain Dew all day because I didn't want all that sugar and caffeine in my system, so I switched my preference to Arnold Palmer's half and half (an ice tea/lemonade combination that has slightly less sugar and caffeine). I could drink a 2-liter container in one day.

It was much easier to rest and heal at home, but it still took time. I could get dizzy and had to wait a few moments sitting in an upright position before I could stand. All my movements had to be in slow motion so I wouldn't fall or accidently bend over. My head needed to stay upright until everything healed properly. I got a long stick with a claw at the end for grabbing things out of reach. I couldn't unload the dishwasher, tie my shoes, or drop my head to spit in the sink after brushing my teeth. Not being allowed to bend, I noticed all the things my kids left on the floor: their coats, books, bags, dishes. I hadn't realized how much picking up I did every day. Our house was a landmine of tripping hazards. After hearing me bark the moment something touched the ground, the kids quickly learned to put their things away.

One day, I stepped on the bathroom scale to access the damage surgery, steroids, and copious amounts of comfort food had done. I gained over 40 pounds. No wonder I could only wear pajama bottoms! I googled the prescription steroid I was prescribed and found nothing good. This wasn't the kind body builders take. It raised blood pressure and blood sugar levels, increased appetite, and caused fat storage in the abdominal region. I didn't want to take this stuff any longer than I had to.

After ten days languishing with greasy hair, I went to the doctor's office and had my staples taken out. I asked about getting off of the steroid and he said I couldn't. It was prescribed to reduce swelling and maintain my sodium levels and he didn't feel comfortable telling me to stop. He said to ask the neurosurgeon when I went for my follow-up appointment in a month. In the meantime I would have to deal with the unfortunate symptoms.

Getting the staples removed dulled the disappointment of having to continue the steroid treatment. I could get the gunk out of my hair. I gently massaged the back of my scalp, shampooing around the newly formed scar across my skull. There is nothing more glorious than the sensation of warm water pouring over your head after weeks of feeling greasy and dirty. I will never forgot how intensely I appreciated that first shower after the staples were removed. As I ran my hand along my head, I felt something hard and crusty, like a scab. Apparently when I was being stapled back together, a couple staples got away. They were shot into my head, more than a few inches from the incision. It's no wonder the nurse missed them when taking out the others. I called the doctor's office and returned to get them taken out before they became a permanent part of my scalp.

After the two weeks ended, my brother flew back home to Seattle and I was on my own. BFF came a couple days a week to keep me company and other visitors stopped by to say hello. Having people come to my house was a huge part of my healing process. As nice as a phone call, email, or letter can be, none of those things have the same impact as a person being physically present with you. I think that is why in an age where technology connects us in so many ways, we feel more disconnected than ever. A written message or phone call leaves us longing for more. Having a person present satisfies and heals. Nothing can replace a shared laugh or hug.

For someone who retreats from people when feeling depressed, having visitors seek me out kept depression at bay. My mind focused on gratitude for these friends instead of self-pity for my circumstances. I appreciated their encouragement and kind words. They told me about people all over the place praying for me and wanting to know how I was doing. They raved about how good I looked, and voiced their relief that my memory returned and my personality remained intact. One friend mentioned someone she knew that had brain surgery and was never quite right afterward.

"I'm really glad you didn't tell me that story before surgery, not that I would have remembered," I replied, chuckling to myself.

"I'm just glad that you are back to your old self," she said with a sigh of relief.

"Me too," I said, thinking of her not-quite-right friend. "Me too."

CHAPTER 13

We can love completely what we cannot completely understand. - Norman Maclean, A River Runs Through It

"Nothing good comes from being normal," says my brother. He should know. He wears non-conformity like a badge of honor. He says he is the black sheep of the family. I have to laugh because as far as I can tell, we are all black sheep, or at the very least, spotted and flawed sheep.

Spending time with my brother was probably the best thing about recovering from surgery. For as long as I can remember, he has been my favorite mystery. Because of our age difference, there have always been parts of him hidden from me. When I was little, he hid behind his music, his role-playing games, and his interest in computers. When he left home and I got older, he drank and used recreational drugs. I lost him for a little while. In time we both matured into our adult selves, yet his interests stayed eclectic: composing music, watching Japanese animation, and gardening. He is like a character in a book that you can never quite pin down. He doesn't fit any pigeon hole one might try to put him in.

There have been times when I think he has worried about me and the person I've become. He talked to me like I grew up to be a conservative, religious fundamentalist, home-schooling mother trapped at home without a life. Our discussions could feel like some kind of political litmus test that I always seemed to flunk. I learned not to antagonize him if I didn't want to listen to an angry, impassioned monologue that lasted until a coughing fit attacked. I loved him but I feared he had turned into a self-absorbed, agonistic teenager trapped in a middle aged body that drank too much coffee and beer, watched Anime, and played video games all day.

I think we were both wrong about each other. You can't really get to know someone from a couple hours of visiting over coffee. Short, sporadic interactions over the course of the last 20 years are all we had to go on. My brother surprised me with his utter selflessness and patience in taking care of me. Even though he remains my favorite mystery, I'd like to think we are more similar than I previously imagined. We don't use the same vocabulary to describe our values, but we believe in the same things.

"I don't believe in anything," Scott said, during one of our discussions that turned to religion.

"We all have values that we believe to be important," I argued. "Different people have different values. Some people value status, higher education, financial success, material wealth, youth, and beauty. You and I don't pursue that stuff. I think we both believe in things like compassion, justice, and integrity."

"That's not what I believe in, that is who I am."

"I know," I told him. "That's how I know we aren't that far apart. We just use different words to say the same thing." That's who I am too, because of Christ in me.

My brother would not credit his goodness to a higher power, but I do. I see what he did for me as God's gracious provision in a restorative package. After feeling orphaned and alone for many years, I feel like I once again have family because my brother took time off of work, spent hours with my 10 year old on her homework, served me water, meals, and medicine at my beck and call, and kept me company when I was as weak and unlovely as one can be. I no longer harbor jealousy toward others that have relationships with their family of origin because now I do too and I give God all the credit.

Even though Scott was just doing what he believed was right, I believe every good and perfect gift comes from above and this reconnection was part of God's plan. My brother believes it is just rational to be a decent human being. There is enough suffering in the world; he doesn't want to intentionally add to it. I would argue that we can't help but add to the suffering. We are human and selfishness comes naturally to us. However, when we act unselfishly with compassion and empathy, we experience the supernatural as we die to our natural selves and live out the goodness that comes from God.

If God exists, He exists whether anyone believes in Him or not. His existence is not dependent on our faith in Him. What is true is true, whether we empirically experience it or not. Just because we haven't physically seen or heard something doesn't mean it isn't there. The earth was round even when ignorant people believed it was flat. There was evidence to point to the truth, but some refused to see it. I believe love is the evidence of God that many refuse to see because they focus on the suffering that He allows to exist, as though the existence of suffering denies the existence of God. It is suffering that reveals the conquering power of love and love's ability to overcome evil with good.

Assuming God exists, He isn't just the God of those who believe in Him, He is the God of the Universe, of everyone. He doesn't love just one group of people because if He is what the Bible claims He is, He is Love, as well as the creator and father of all nations. There are no distinctions, no classes of people in God's eyes. God loves even those who don't believe in Him. In fact, he pursues them, like a shepherd tracking a lost sheep. And He uses them for His purposes because He can. When my brother said he has never heard or seen God, I couldn't help but say, "Look around you! These people. This food. This is God."

What I saw as a witness to God's existence and provision, Scott saw as evidence of my involvement in the community. I guess everything I see as proof of the divine can be explained by other means, but that doesn't keep me from hoping I'm right. I hope that

God's promises are true and one day sickness and death will be destroyed and all things will be made new again.

My brother may be a rational agnostic, but God still works through him for His glory. Being in a position that required constant care humbled me but it was worth it to see God in my mysterious brother. God gave me the beauty of my brother's love for the ashes of my weakened condition.

CHAPTER 14

The Spirit is indeed willing, but the flesh is weak. – Matthew 26:41

Those first few months after surgery, my body felt tired and achy most of the time, but my brain buzzed with activity. I didn't know what a fantastic memory I had until it was gone and when I got it back I was filled with so much gratitude and exuberance, I wanted to use all my untapped potential. I had ideas for a presentation on the weaknesses of standard care practices in hospitals, a concert with a detailed testimony of my journey, and an outline for a book I would write. I had aspirations to be like Tony Robbins and become an inspirational life coach. There was so much to share and I wanted to start right away!

Unfortunately, my body did not want to cooperate. I worked for an hour organizing our household files and I needed to take a nap. I dropped the kids off at school and came home exhausted. I didn't even have to do anything and I felt tired. My mind and body were at war with each other. One wanted to take on the world and the other wanted to do as little as possible. I tried to be patient but when I explained how I felt to my doctors in Seattle, it was as though I was talking to myself.

I went to my follow-up appointments in June. The surgeon and his head resident patted themselves on the back for the great job they did on my surgery, pleased with my beautifully healing scar and lack of neurological complications. When I tried to tell them that I wasn't feeling as good as I looked, they brushed me off. The scar looked good. The endocrinology team would handle the hormone related issues. I would have to take my concerns up with them.

I visited endocrinology next. I lamented that I felt fat, tired, and unmotivated. "You're still healing. Give it time," was the pat response I received. The endocrinology resident instructed me to continue my course of steroids in order to maintain my cortisol levels. When I asked about my thyroid, he asked if I was losing my hair or having problems with constipation. I wasn't. Despite having other symptoms, he didn't pursue any course of treatment. Blood tests showed my thyroid levels were within a normal range.

I mentioned my incredible thirst and inability to sleep through the night.

"Are you wakened by thirst?"

"I wake up having to go to the bathroom and I'm thirsty too."

"That can improve over time. Let's wait and see if it improves on its own."

I left that day in no better position than when I arrived. The resident ordered blood tests to be taken six weeks later to monitor my progress and said he would call with the results. Weeks passed and he never called. In the meantime, I continued to drink like a camel, pee like a racehorse, and sleep like a cat.

It dawned on me that all the times I judged people for being fat and lazy, it never occurred to me that they weren't living that way on purpose. I figured the world is full of Type As, the builders and doers who get things done, and Type Bs, who daydream, doodle and depend on the work of others. I disliked those B people. They were the mooching grasshoppers that expected to benefit from the fruits of the ants' labor. Yet, here I was an A mind trapped in B body. I wanted to be a doer, but all I had the energy for was daydreaming and doodling. I couldn't help it. I started feeling sympathy and mercy for those without an ambition gland. It seemed like mine had been removed.

I called the doctor's office in Seattle and the receptionist told me the doctor I visited was no longer there. No one else had been assigned my case. It was assumed I would receive continued care at home, even though I told them we only had one endocrinologist in town and her appointment calendar was booked for months. The receptionist offered to schedule an appointment with another provider but I could only be seen on a Thursday morning, during clinic hours. An office visit would require an overnight stay during the middle of the week. "Never mind," I said and I hung up.

A couple days later, my cell phone rang during a library volunteer meeting. I looked at the caller id and it was the local clinic. I quickly walked to the lobby and answered the call. "Sarah, this is Dr. H. I was looking over your blood tests. Were you able to get an appointment to see the specialist in Seattle?"

"I called and he isn't even there anymore. He left a couple weeks ago and no one even looked at my test results."

"I will call the local specialist and get you in. You are too important to fall through the cracks."

His comment caught me off guard. Maybe he meant to say, "THIS is too important to fall through the cracks" but I distinctly heard "YOU." It struck me as the kindest thing a doctor has ever said to me. I had begun to think no one in the medical profession cared how I felt, that I had fallen through the cracks. My lack of motivation extended to my vigilance in taking care of myself and I was ready to give up. That phone call startled me and woke me from my despondency. It reminded me that I am worth the effort and there are some caring doctors in the world. I was fortunate enough to have more than one.

The local endocrinologist saw me within the week. She spent over an hour explaining the functions of the pituitary gland, how it regulates all the hormones of the body, and why I felt the way I did. She ordered a stress test to determine whether or not I needed to continue taking a steroid. If I stopped and my body didn't produce its own in the appropriate levels, I would not be able to get out of bed. She gave me a prescription for a medicine to regulate fluid control since it had been months since the surgery and it hadn't improved on its own. She also started me on thyroid medication as my blood test showed my levels had decreased since surgery. Once I passed the stress test, she took me off of the steroid and monitored my thyroid, increasing the dosage as needed.

"Will this make me lose weight?" I wanted desperately for her to say yes.

"Thyroid medication is not prescribed for weight loss. You may lose some weight, but it will take time and you will need to diet and exercise. If you start to get jittery or can't get to sleep, let me know. It may mean that this is too high of a dose and we will need to reduce it."

I asked more questions about the kind of diet she recommended and what changes I could expect. All the while, I secretly wanted to feel jittery. It had been so long since I felt that excited feeling caffeine gives when you aren't immune to it. To have the energy to stay up all night and clean tile grout or alphabetize my spice rack sounded like a dream. I know that sounds crazy, but it had been so long since I had the energy to do anything. I missed being able to be neurotic if the mood hit me.

In time, I gradually started feeling better. I went for walks in the evening with my neighbor and gradually eased back into the household chores like cooking and laundry. One Saturday, my daughter Lauren said to me, "Mom, you're doing really well today. You haven't taken a single nap and it's almost 3pm." I never thought I'd measure my progress by the number of naps I required, but I counted it as a victory, no matter how small.

In August, four months after my surgery, I had an MRI to monitor the remnant of the tumor that had been left behind. The sticky little gob wouldn't budge and had to be monitored. This particular type of tumor, though non-cancerous, has a tendency to grow back. The endocrinologist I visited assured me that I was in no immediate danger and I could take my time in deciding what course of treatment to take if the tumor grew back. She speculated that radiation would cause permanent and irreversible damage to my pituitary gland and suggested I get a second opinion from another specialist if the team in Seattle recommended radiation after surgery. Her advice sounded good at the time but I couldn't take her with me to the consult with the radiation oncologist. I was on my own, outnumbered and outgunned.

CHAPTER 15

Radiation is not pleasant. – Farrah Fawcett

Since Ben hated traveling in the city and I hated traveling with him, he let me go to my consultation with the radiation oncologist in Seattle alone. It had been five months since my surgery and I could finally get through the day without spontaneously falling asleep. I gave myself plenty of time to stop and rest if needed. The drive was uneventful and I arrived with enough time to have lunch with my brother and his friend before my appointment.

This was my first time visiting Harborview Medical Center. Though part of the University of Washington Medical System, Harborview looked nothing like the University hospital where I had surgery. Situated on a hill overlooking downtown, the art deco style building stood ominous and bleak, surrounded by other medical office buildings and public housing projects. It looked like what it was: an old, utilitarian inter-city hospital where ambulances drop off drug addicts that overdose, crime victims with gunshot wounds, and people injured in car accidents. The radiology department was housed on the windowless first floor, down a sterile, artless hallway.

My brother and his friend came with me to the appointment and helped pass the time as we waited for the doctor to arrive. I read old magazines until a nurse came to enter my intake information: height, weight, blood pressure, and health history. Fifteen minutes after she left, two medical students arrived to talk to me. They timidly explained that the portion of the tumor left behind after surgery was beginning to develop cysts. They went over three different kinds of radiation treatment and the positives and negatives of each option. Then, with hesitation, they asked what my thoughts were.

I thought about what my doctor at home had said about not rushing into a decision and I told them I wasn't really interested in radiation right now. School would be starting soon. Fall could be a busy time for my family. I didn't want to be incapacitated again after just starting to feel better. The medical students mumbled something to each other and left the room. After another ten minutes, the doctor arrived. He wasn't as academic or timid as the students had been. He let me have it.

"I don't think you understand the severity of your situation," he said firmly. "If we wait and the cyst interferes with your optic nerve or frontal lobe like before, radiation will no longer be an option. You could lose your vision, permanently. We need to act while the cystic component remains small because it has the potential to grow rapidly and cause irreversible damage. Not only that, if it continues to grow, it could require another surgery. You don't want to do that again, do you?"

"No….but what about my pituitary gland? Won't radiation damage it?" I asked.

"It could. But all those hormones are replaceable. Your vision isn't," he said, speaking like someone who wasn't having his hormones replaced. "We need to take care of this right away."

"Sound like I don't have much choice in the matter," I responded.

"Not if you want to avoid the consequences of doing nothing," the doctor said firmly.

He explained what would need to happen before treatment began. I would need to go to a dentist and get fitted for a special mouthpiece. This mouthpiece would lock into the roof of my mouth and attach to a cage that would hold my head perfectly still. With my head locked into position, an exacting laser of radiation would target the specific point where the largest cyst originated. This "knife" of gamma rays would kill those cells and over time the cyst would gradually shrink away.

The hospital scheduled me to return for pre-treatment preparation in three weeks with gamma knife radiation starting in a little over one month. I would receive five treatments over five days, fifteen minutes each visit. Fortunately for me, my brother's apartment was eight blocks away from the hospital and he was willing to let me stay with him and his wife during my week of treatment. I just needed to make arrangements for my two return trips and clear my schedule.

I drove home over the mountains with a feeling of numb resignation. The appointment didn't go the way I had planned. I didn't want the radiation, its side effects, and the risk of cancer later in life, but what choice did I have? I didn't have the time or resources to seek another opinion. I would have to drive to Portland or fly to Minneapolis and pay for a consultation out of my own pocket. My insurance plan wouldn't cover appointments with doctors out of their network. After all the expenses I had already incurred from my surgery, prescriptions, and MRIs, we just couldn't afford to spend more money with the possibility I would get the same advice. I decided to close those doors and trust that everything would work out for the best. I wanted to keep my sight and sanity, so I resolved to do what the expert in Seattle recommended.

I returned home and continued life as usual. I cooked healthy meals and watched what I ate, but at night I craved bread and cereal. I ate toast and jam or oatmeal before going to bed and got mad at myself in the morning. At least the cool fall weather helped me to get out of the house and move more. Carolyn started a paper route in a neighborhood about a half mile from our house. After school, I drove her to the start of her route and helped her deliver papers. It was a good way to ease into daily exercise. I started running again, but it felt like I was carrying a four-year-old on my back. Because I had gained so much weight, my knees ached after only a short jog. I got winded and out of breathe even though I was jogging slower than

my old easy pace. I remembered that it had been rough when I
started running the first time, but I didn't remember it being like this.
I felt defeated and frustrated. I decided if I ever did write a book
about my experience, I would call it "I'm Mad My Brain Tumor
Made Me Fat."

For the first time in their lives, both girls went to public school
all day, every day, leaving me with extra time to myself at home.
Before my surgery, the cable company called and offered a special on
installation. Not being in my right mind, I agreed. We had never had
cable television before but I was happy to have it during this season.
It kept me entertained when I couldn't get off the couch and kept me
company while the girls were away at school. Not having them with
me all the time made me realize just how much I enjoyed being with
them. Missing them during the day made me appreciate our time
together more. Lauren even said, "I love weekends so much more
now because they are like the way every day used to be before we
went to school."

"Yeah. Every day used to be a weekend. We were lucky," I
reminisced with her. I lacked the energy and inclination to go back
to homeschooling, but I felt thankful every day that we did it for as
long as we had.

I had one short trip to Seattle before my week-long stay for
radiation treatment. I drove to Olympia and stayed with my friend
Carol, who I met when I worked as a volunteer at a Crisis Pregnancy
Center around the time Ben and I were first married. We kept in

touch after I moved around the country with Ben's job in the military. When Ben and I moved back to Washington and he started his job at Key Technology in Walla Walla, she told us her younger brother worked there too. Now she had two families to visit in our town and when she came to see her brother, she would stop and see us too.

I wasn't looking forward to driving in Seattle alone, so Carol volunteered to drive me there. She offered to let me stay with her before and after my day of pre-treatment appointments so I wouldn't have to worry about getting around town by myself. During our break between appointments, she took me to a high-end grocery store in West Seattle to spy on her competition. She managed a grocery store in Olympia with a similar style of deli and gift department. It was fun seeing a store through the eyes of management and I appreciated her taking the time to be my companion. Just like my friend Kathy did on the day before surgery, Carol helped me keep my mind on positive thoughts of friendship and healing.

I went home and a week later flew to Seattle. I didn't have to rent a car because the commuter rail runs directly from the airport to downtown. I loved being at ease on the train instead of feeling tense and stressed navigating through traffic. I closed my eyes and imagined that I was going on a five day retreat, a time to relax and unwind. Less than an hour of each day would be spent at the hospital so I tried to focus on the time I wouldn't be there.

My first treatment on Monday was scheduled in the afternoon, giving me time to arrive in the city. The following treatments would all be first thing in the morning at 8am. I was instructed to wear loose, comfortable clothing and bring calming music the staff could play during the treatment. They found it helped patients remain still. I brought the only classical music I own, the Onyx Chamber Players performing Mozart's Piano Quartet in E major and Shostakovich's Piano Trio op.67. The pianist is the husband of a friend from high school. If I need help falling asleep, it is my go-to music.

The staff helped me onto the long platform and positioned my body so my head would fit perfectly into the frame. They slid the rubber and plastic mouth piece into my mouth and praised me for only gagging once. I slowly laid down and the technician snapped the mouthpiece into the arms of the head frame. She slid cushions along either ear, packing me like a fragile gift being shipped in a box. She put a small box with a button and cord in my hand and said, "If you feel frightened or uncomfortable, push this button. We'll stop everything and won't start again until you feel better."

Finally, a radiologist and the oncologist came into the room and took measurements of some kind, lining points on my head with points on the frame. They moved my shoulders very slightly until they felt I was perfectly aligned. The doctor said over and over, "You're doing great. Thank you for being so still. Everything is going so smoothly." His encouragement made me feel like a schoolgirl wanting to please her teacher. I didn't dare touch the button in my hand because I hated the thought of making everyone do all this work over again. I liked that they were happy with me. I'm sure experts have run experiments on patients to study the effects of constant affirmations. They worked for me.

Everyone left the room and the platform moved slightly. Unlike an MRI, my body didn't slide into a capsule. I couldn't see any part of the radiation machine from where I laid. I heard a voice from the overhead speaker say, "We're going to get started. It will take about 15 minutes. We will let you know when you're finished and come in to help you. We'll start your music now." I closed my eyes and wondered if swallowing the spit pooling in my mouth would cause my head to move at all. I decided that if it did, it wouldn't be the part that was getting radiated, so I took my chances. I prayed that God would keep me from gagging or feeling like I was choking. After a few tense moments, I relaxed and listened to the music. I thought of dancing fingers on the piano keys and rocking bows gliding back and forth on the violin strings. I was almost asleep when the music stopped and a voice overhead said, "All done. We'll be in there shortly."

The doors to the room opened and the staff entered as the bed moved forward. The nurse released my head from the stabilizing cage. I sat upright and wiggled the handle of the mouthpiece to release its suction to the roof of my mouth and slowly pulled it out. I gagged a little and the nurse handed me a small towel to hold over my mouth and wipe my face. I turned to get off the table and she held my arm as I stepped down to the floor.

"That went very well. I like your music selection," the doctor said. "We'll see you in the morning and do this all over again." I gathered my coat and purse from the chair near the wall.

"What time should I come?" I asked.

"Be here by 8am and we'll get started as soon as we can."

The next morning I left my brother's apartment at 7:30am and arrived at the hospital a few minutes before eight. The doctor arrived around 8:30am. I finished thumbing through two People Magazines and an Us Weekly. The nurse came into the room where I was waiting and brought me a cup of water and a pill. "This is a steroid to prevent inflammation and swelling."

"Do I have to take it?" I hated the idea of taking steroids again. She left and returned with the doctor.

"I hear you aren't crazy about taking a steroid. Take one today. We'll give you a half dose tomorrow and if you don't have any discomfort or symptoms, you may not need to take anymore." he explained.

Each morning for four days the process was repeated. Before I left on Friday, the doctor explained that in a couple weeks, I would feel the effects of radiation: loss of appetite, nausea, headaches, body aches, and fatigue. In short, I would feel like I got hit by a semi-truck. Luckily, for the week of treatment, I felt fine and had a wonderful time enjoying Seattle.

I arrived back at Scott's apartment around the same time he returned from working the opening shift at Starbucks. Each morning he took me to a different café for breakfast and at night, we tried a variety of ethnic foods. We visited Glo's on Capitol Hill and Geraldine's Counter in Columbia City. One day, we took the bus to Redmond and ate lunch with my sister-in-law Monica at the Microsoft Campus. I had butter chicken from the Indian café. I had never eaten it before but I figured anything that has the word butter in the title couldn't taste bad and it didn't disappoint. It was delicious.

We also hunted for the best cupcakes in town. We tried Cupcake Royale on Pike Street and the Yellow Leaf Cupcake company downtown on 4th Street. Cupcake Royale made a treat with whiskey and bacon that caught Scott's attention. I tried the Caramel apple. It tasted delightful going down but landed in my gut like a brick. The almond cake from Yellow Leaf lacked the vibrant sweetness of its competitor but it didn't make me sick later so it was my winner.

Opera Girl came to the city on her day off and spent the day with me after my treatment on Wednesday. We played tourist, stopping at the garden in Volunteer Park, eating seafood at Ivar's, and touring the Theo chocolate factory. We visited the Troll under the Fremont Bridge and window shopped downtown before having a light dinner of appetizers at McCormick & Schmick's. We filled every moment of the day and I didn't once feel the need to stop for a nap but I did sleep like a rock that night.

By the time I took the train back to the airport on Friday afternoon, I was ready to return home to my family and resume life as normal. That lasted about ten days. Then, the doctor's prediction came true and I got hit by the Mack truck of radiation treatment. Normal as I knew it would never be seen or heard from again.

CHAPTER 16

Normal is nothing more than a cycle on a
washing machine. - Whoopi Goldberg

Two months later in December, I went to the local hospital for a new MRI.

"So, is this a follow-up scan?" asked the radiology technician.

"Yeah. I finished radiation treatment a couple months ago and they are checking to see what's happened to my brain tumor since then."

She helped me lay back into the mold for my head and helped me scoot into position. "How have you been feeling?"

"A couple weeks after treatment, I felt like complete garbage, but I'm feeling better now. I'm taking medicine to replace the hormones that went missing and I'm starting to feel human again. I'm giving myself until April to get back to my old normal," I told her in a hopeful tone. Recovering from radiation treatment felt like having a prolonged illness like mononucleosis. I was happy if I could get through an hour long television show without falling asleep. My muscles hurt when I got out of bed and ached when I returned at night.

What gave me hope was the knowledge that I was on a journey to wellness and I hadn't arrived yet. It was a little like climbing the mountains at Silver Falls State Park. I had to tell myself, "Just keep swimming," like I did while I ran that damp, dark marathon the year before. Eventually, this season of recovery would be a memory, just like that run, and I was determined to do everything in my power to get to the place where I felt healthy and whole again.

"You may want to adjust to a new normal," the technician said as she stuffed cushioning alongside each of my ears. She looked at me with pity in her eyes as if I was a sad little puppy.

"I'm still in a relationship with Old Normal. I have feelings for him and I'm not ready to break up," I explained to her.

New Normal was not welcome to stay. If Old Normal looked like a Subaru commercial, New Normal looked like a commercial for Zoloft. I wanted to be active outdoors with Old Normal and go white water rafting and body surfing. I had no desire to trade the old life of fun for a new life of falling asleep while reading. I feared feeling slow and tired forever, growing morbidly obese and unable to leave my couch. I was too young for that and wasn't willing to accept a new normal if that's where it would take me.

The technician smiled and chuckled. "Well, good luck with that. If it doesn't work out, don't be too hard on yourself. You did have brain surgery."

"Thanks for reminding me," I mutter under my breath as the machine slid me into the imaging coffin for my MRI. I knew she was trying to be kind, but being told to accept my body and my life the way it was angered me. I felt like my identity had been stolen from me and I was supposed to be okay with it and not fight back. I wasn't willing to do that.

I pushed myself to return to my old habit of jogging at night, forcing myself to put on running shoes and get out the front door. I had to prove to myself that I could still be the same person I was before surgery. It wasn't easy and I couldn't look to the scale for any encouragement. All the extra weight I gained over the year made running hard on my knees, feet, and ego. I bought better shoes, continued to train, and lost five pounds in four months of running four days a week.

My pituitary gland was like the guy who shows up to work, but doesn't actually do anything. He stopped sending messages to my thyroid gland, which pretty much shriveled up like a piece of dried fruit. I had the dosage of synthetic hormone increased three times over the course of a few months. That helped a lot. It's amazing how getting my hormones back in balance changed my energy level and attitude.

I had my ambition back. I didn't have to nap to get through the day and I could run without feeling like I was carrying another person on my back. By April, I was ready to show that a brain tumor couldn't keep me down. I ran the Spokane River Run 10K trail run, tromping through rocks, trees, and fields. I stopped for a few walk breaks but sprinted the last quarter mile and crossed the finish line feeling ready to do it again. It felt wonderful to know that my debilitating fatigue wasn't a life sentence.

From the outside, it looked as though my old normal was back. As my husband said, "You like to live your life at a certain pace. You are pretty much at the same pace you were before." I was back to running, working multiple part-time jobs, and volunteering in the community. Yet, on the inside, I felt different. This journey from memory loss to brain surgery and recovery changed me. Though my personality and lifestyle stayed the same, my heart and mind did not. It took being weak and admitting I was broken to find my strength and learn what it means to be whole.

CHAPTER 17

God whispers to us in our pleasures, speaks to us
in our conscious, but shouts to us in our pains:
It is His megaphone to rouse a deaf world.
– C.S. Lewis

As strange as it may seem, I'm glad this all happened. I never want to get my head cut open ever again and I pray that I don't have to get radiation treatment again either. However, the process revealed so many false assumptions I had about my identity, my relationships, and my reality that I wouldn't want to go back to the person I used to be. I had been staring at shadows on a cave wall, thinking I understood how life worked. The process of discovering my brain tumor and treating it turned my head to the cave opening and surprised me with all its revelations. The hidden Matrix has been exposed and I've been set free from a prison I didn't know was holding me. This new normal isn't what I thought it was and I don't want to go back to the old one.

Before the brain tumor, I felt good about my efforts to create a happy life. Freed from the chaos and insecurity I experienced as a child, I focused on being dependable and responsible for my family as an adult. I centered my life on my home and my community, devoting myself to the people and ideals that mattered most to me. I enjoyed being admired for my leadership and organizational skills and spent time on activities that allowed those parts of me to shine. My identity rested on my ability to be everything I thought a woman should be. I thought I knew what mattered in life, but I was terribly wrong.

Somewhere along the way, I got the idea that my worth depended on my appearance and productivity. My greatest fear was to be thought of as ugly, fat, or lazy so I did everything I could to avoid being those things. I exercised, dieted, and obsessed about my weight and waistline. When I wasn't thinking about my physical appearance, I turned my attention to the appearance of my home and family. Even though I wasn't consciously trying to impress or compete with other families, I constantly compared myself to them. I needed some kind of outside validation that I was doing it right, whatever it was. I just wanted to feel whole and no matter what I did, I felt inadequate.

In making my identity and value all about being a wife and mother, I lost who I was, and I did my family a huge disservice as well. I treated them like my work instead of my people, turning my joy into drudgery. I measured my worth by the work I did for them and their acknowledgement. If they were happy, I felt good. If they were unhappy, I took it personally, as though it was a reflection on me and my performance. I acted like a genie in a bottle, waiting to grant wishes or answer commands, resenting the people I wanted to love. I looked like a good mother on the outside, but I often felt like a failure.

Losing my memory and my competence made me realize that my identity reaches deeper than the superficial level of roles and jobs. No matter what is going on with my mind or my health, my true identity is God's masterpiece. He is working in me to make me the woman He wants me to be and like clay, I am being molded and shaped. Part of that shaping was breaking my need to be productive and praised in order to feel worthy. It took losing the capability to be what I thought a mom and wife should be for me to realize my intrinsic value is independent of my family and what I do in my home. My Creator loves me, accepts me, and plans good things for me to do.

When God broke my need for competency, He put my ego and family in their proper place, subordinate to His plan. Part of His plan was for me to love and care for my family, without strings or reservations. My family loves me desperately and they appreciate me, but their approval does not determine my value or worth. It's not my family's job to massage my ego and it's not my job to make all their dreams come true. We are called to love each other and take responsibility for our attitudes and actions without blaming others. God gave me these people as a gift to enjoy and I enjoy them more now because I don't make everything they do and say about me.

Seeing myself in this new light reoriented my relationship with my husband and my children. As a friend once said, "A right relationship with God makes your relationships with people right too." I cherish our time together. Waking in the morning, I remind myself that none of us are guaranteed another day. I think to myself, "If this was our last day together, how would I treat them?" With that in mind, I want the last word I say to my family members to be a loving one, not impatient or angry. I want whatever memory they have of the last time they saw me to be a good one. I make an effort to give hugs and kisses at departures and time and attention at arrivals.

My husband and I spend more time together now. Because he was so scared of losing me, my husband is more willing to enter my world and do banal stuff with me, like running errands or grocery shopping. We make dinner together instead of spending time in separate rooms. We schedule date nights or evening walks. It's easy to forget we are more than partners in the business of raising a family. We are each other's champion, retirement plan, and greatest asset. We are lucky to have each other, to have the time we've been given. I'm lucky to have a family to love. Without love, all the work in the world is meaningless.

As much as I hate to admit it, having me sidelined for a while was good for my kids. I'm happy that I've been able to give them what I missed when I was growing up, but I never intended to rob them of the independence and responsibility I had. Fortunately, I got to see firsthand that the more responsibility they are given, the more they thrive. They are capable of taking care of their clothes, their lunches, and their home. It's not unreasonable to ask that they make their beds and do their dishes. They can pack sack lunches, wipe down counters, and sweep floors. While I buzzed around the house, making it magazine ready, they were watching. I'm delighted to know that when they have their own homes, I won't have to come over to clean. They know how.

Getting sidelined was good for me, too. My greatest source of pain wasn't the tumor, the surgery, or the radiation treatment; it was my broken ego. It took losing my ability to work or even wash my hair for me to realize that no one loves me for my productivity or good looks. Even sick, ugly, and unable to get off the couch, my family still loved me for who I am to them, not what I do for them or how I look. Paul wrote to the Galatians, "You were running the race so well. Who has held you back from following the truth?" I was held back by subconsciously believing the lie that how I looked and what people thought of me was what mattered most. It chained me in discontent and distracted me from the life God intended for me to live.

Vanity still tries to convince me that I'm not thin enough, not athletic enough, not pretty enough, but it is a liar. I learned that whether running a marathon or recovering from surgery, I need to closely monitor the voice in my head. I want to live in the truth of God's grace and redemptive work in my life and not believe the lies of pride and vanity. I don't need to prove anything to anyone, including myself. I just need to be fully alive, present in the moment, and appreciate the opportunities I have to serve and love others. I don't need to be as thin or as fast or as energetic as I was before. There is nothing I need to do to be whole, loved, and accepted. I just have to believe I am and rest in that knowledge. I am enough, without exception.

I'm less afraid of people now, less afraid of being evaluated and found lacking. Most comments and suggestions people make are not intended to be personal attacks. If they are, it's not a reflection on me, but the speaker's own insecurities. The vast majority of people in my life wish me well and deserve my trust and respect. I don't need to fear unsolicited advice and I gain nothing if I let sensitivity keep me from learning from the wisdom and experience of others.

This journey has shown me how numb and isolated I had made myself. I preferred to keep my own company and be alone rather than risk anxiety and social rejection. I convinced myself that the arms-length at which I kept people was close enough. I guarded my heart against criticism and judgment, I ignored my own weakness, and I tried to pretend I could protect myself from suffering and pain. I was willing to help others, but unwilling to seek help for myself. With my mind focused on my image and performance, I locked myself in a prison of solitary confinement, unwilling to let anyone in.

Because of my condition, my need overpowered my pride

and my eyes were opened to the gift of community that surrounded me. A sweater of connection was knitted around my family. Christianity became more than a personal faith as people generously displayed the truth and beauty of God's grace. They bore my burdens and fulfilled the law of Christ by blessing my family with food, prayer, money, and personal support. They loved me when I was my most unlovable and proved to me that my faith is true. God is love and His love is what makes life worthwhile.

"Dear friends, let us continue to love one another, for love comes from God. Anyone who loves is born of God and knows God. But anyone who does not love does not know God – for God is love." I John 4:7-8 NLT

After my first half-marathon, May '12   After brain surgery, April '13

Radiation week with Scott, Oct '13

ABOUT THE AUTHOR

Sarah Bergman lives in Walla Walla, WA with her husband, Benjamin, and two daughters, Lauren and Carolyn. She continues to run, lead 4-H youth, and enjoy the company of friends and family. She works part-time for the Walla Walla Valley Medical Society and Book and Game Company.

58413043R00106

Made in the USA
Charleston, SC
10 July 2016